M. J. GROVER

Metal Detecting Gold Nuggets

The Essential Guide to Finding Gold with a Metal Detector

First edition

ISBN: 978-1-7362750-5-4

This book was professionally typeset on Reedsy.
Find out more at reedsy.com

Contents

Introduction

This book will teach you the skills needed to go out and successfully find gold with a metal detector. While there's no comparison to getting out in the field and learning first hand, the knowledge presented in this book will get you started on your hunt.

Note that terms like "gold detectorist," "electronic prospector," "nugget shooter," "nugget hunter," or "gold hunter," are all used interchangeably in this book to describe a person who uses a metal detector to find gold nuggets.

A Brief History of Gold Prospecting

Gold prospecting around the world has has a rich and fascinating history, filled with tales of discovery, booms, and the pursuit of the precious metal that has captivated the human imagination for centuries.

Gold has been valued around the world. Ancient gold relics have been found in the Indus Valley (present-day India and Pakistan), Mesopotamia (present-day Iraq), Egypt, China, Greece, and throughout Central and South America that date back thousands of years.

In more recent history here in the United States, gold mining has been taking place for roughly 200 years. Here are a few key milestones in the history of gold mining in the U.S.:

Early U.S. Gold Discoveries:

Eastern U.S.:

- 1799: The first documented discovery of gold in the United States occurs in North Carolina, when a 17-pound gold nugget is found in Cabarrus County.
- 1828: Gold is discovered in Lumpkin County, Georgia, starting the first major gold rush in the eastern United States. Additional gold deposits would soon be discovered in Alabama, South Carolina, Virginia, and other eastern states.

California Gold Rush:

- 1848: Gold is discovered at Sutter's Mill in Coloma, triggering the famous California Gold Rush.
- Thousands of prospectors from all over the world flock to California in search of gold, leading to rapid population growth and the development of towns and cities.
- The California Gold Rush transforms the region, shapes its economy, and plays a significant role in the westward expansion of the United States.

Other Major Gold Rushes:

- 1859: The Pike's Peak Gold Rush takes place in Colorado, drawing prospectors seeking their fortunes in the Rocky Mountains.
- Late 1800s: Gold rushes occur in various other regions, including Nevada (Comstock Lode), Idaho (Boise Basin), Montana (Last Chance Gulch), and Alaska and the Yukon Territory (Klondike Gold Rush).

Industrialization and Consolidation:

- Late 1800s: As gold mining becomes more industrialized, larger corporations and mining companies begin to dominate the industry.
- Mining techniques advance, with the introduction of hydraulic mining, dredging, and underground mining methods. Most small-scale prospectors have moved on to other ventures.

Decline and Modern Gold Prospecting:

- Early 1900s: Many of the major gold rushes decline. Small-scale prospecting has a slight resurgence during the Great Depression, but for the most the era of individual prospectors making their living from gold mining is over. Most gold mined in the U.S. comes from a relatively small group of very large mining operations.

- Despite the decline, gold prospecting continues to be pursued by individuals, hobbyists, and small-scale miners across the country. Most miners use placer mining equipment like gold pans, sluice boxes and suction dredges.

- Around 1980, the first metal detector capable of consistently finding gold was produced. The Garrett Goldhog ran at a higher frequency than other coin detectors, and limited ground canceling abilities made it possible to use it successfully in the goldfields. Combined with the escalating price of gold during this time started a modern "electronic gold rush" that continues to this day.

This old advertisement is from 1965. Certainly a detector like this might find a huge nugget right at the surface, but I doubt it could handle the mineralized soils commonly found in the goldfields.

The Rise of Electronic Prospecting

The arrival of the Garrett Groundhog was a pivotal moment in gold prospecting history. No longer was there a need for the backbreaking work of shoveling gravel through a sluice box or digging tunnels into the Earth chasing a vein of gold. Gold could now be found simply by scanning the ground to locate targets.

This also allowed prospectors to quickly explore new areas quickly. New discoveries were made, and areas once considered to be exhausted or "mined out" were revisited with success.

The rise of electronic gold prospecting, particularly the use of metal detectors for finding gold nuggets, has revolutionized the field of gold prospecting in recent decades.

Metal detectors, initially designed for industrial and military purposes, started gaining popularity in the mid-20th century for recreational treasure hunting. Technological advancements beginning in the 1980s improved metal detector circuitry, sensitivity, and target discrimination, making them more suitable for gold prospecting.

These early detectors weren't fancy. They would miss most of the smaller targets and couldn't located nuggets very deep in the ground, but they worked well enough on larger gold close to the surface. Many goldfields were hiding incredible amounts of gold like this, and it was easy pickin' for those first electronic prospectors. The use of metal detectors allowed areas to be effectively searched in ways that other methods simply couldn't do.

Throughout the 1980s and 1990s, more specialized metal detectors designed specifically for gold prospecting were introduced, offering improved sensitivity and discrimination features.

The availability of dedicated gold prospecting metal detectors led to the widespread adoption of electronic gold prospecting among enthusiasts and professional prospectors.

Online communities, forums, and dedicated websites emerged, facilitating knowledge sharing and fostering a community of electronic gold prospecting enthusiasts. Success stories have certainly helped increase interest as well.

The rise of electronic gold prospecting had transformed the field, allowing prospectors to efficiently and accurately detect gold nuggets, opening up new possibilities for exploration and discovery.

The First Gold Detectors

Garrett Groundhog:

Released in 1980, the Garrett Groundhog was the first gold prospecting metal detector. It provided improved sensitivity to gold nuggets and had adjustable ground balance settings to minimize interference from mineralized soils.

Original Fisher Gold Bug:

Introduced in the late 1980s, the Fisher Gold Bug was one of the first metal detectors specifically designed for gold prospecting. It offered high sensitivity to small gold nuggets and featured manual ground balancing to handle mineralized soil conditions. The Gold Bug quickly became one of the most popular detectors of its time.

Whites Goldmaster Series:

Whites Electronics introduced the Goldmaster series to great fanfare. Older models under the Goldmaster name were marketed even back as far as the 1960s, but later models were true gold-getters. The Goldmaster models offered specialized features for gold prospecting, such as high-frequency operation and ground balance adjustment, making them effective tools for finding gold nuggets.

Tesoro Lobo SuperTRAQ:

The Tesoro Lobo SuperTRAQ, released in the late 1990s, became known for its ability to detect small gold nuggets. It featured automatic ground tracking and a high operating frequency, optimizing its performance in gold-rich areas.

Minelab SD Series:

In the mid-1990s, Minelab launched its SD series of metal detectors, including the SD2000, SD2100, and SD2200. These detectors gained popularity among gold prospectors due to their enhanced sensitivity to small gold nuggets and advanced ground tracking capabilities. These detectors truly revolutionized electronic prospecting by incorporating a new technology that was superior at eliminating ground noise. They could detect gold nuggets at extreme depths that other detectors were not capable of.

Advancements have continued and still continue to this day. There are several different companies manufacturing both gold-specific and multi-use type detectors that are highly capable of finding gold nuggets. We will discuss these in the next chapter.

Opportunities for the Modern Electronic Prospector

There is good and bad news for the modern-day electronic prospector. While specialized gold detectors continue to improve, this means that the popular goldfields have been hunted hard now. Areas that were once "easy pickin'" for a prospector using these older metal detectors are now thoroughly hunted. Many areas have now been heavily depleted of detectable gold.

With electronic prospectors now searching some of these areas for over 40 years, big gold nuggets near the surface are long gone. In most areas, only the hard to find nuggets are left;

- Small gold nuggets
- Deep nuggets
- gold/quartz specimens
- nuggets obscured by iron trash

Even with the most advanced detectors, finding gold can be a real challenge in many areas. Throughout this book, we will discuss techniques and tactics to make you a successful nugget hunter in this modern environment. Finding gold nuggets has always been a challenging endeavor, but skilled technique is more important than ever if you want to be successful.

Even in the 2020s and beyond, a skilled metal detectorist can go out and successfully find gold nuggets with a metal detector.

Choosing a Metal Detector

There are hundreds of different types of handheld metal detectors on the market today. They range in prices from less than $100 up to over $8,000. But price is hardly the only consideration to need to consider when choosing a metal detector. In fact, only a small percentage of the modern metal detectors made today are capable of finding gold nuggets with any consistency.

Most metal detectors on the market are made to find coins. Coins present a big, solid target. Most of the time, their intended use is in areas with fairly consistent ground types like parks, ball fields, or sandy beaches.

Gold nuggets are rarely found in these types of areas. Instead, gold is almost always found in locations with highly mineralized ground and high iron content. The ground can be highly variable. One sweep of the detector coil might scan over pockets of black sands comprised of hematite or magnetite, chunks of solid quartz, serpentine, slate, granite, or a wide array of mineral types all in the same small area.

All this variation will cause the average metal detector to struggle, resulting in chatter and ground noise that will mask the sound of gold nuggets in the ground. A good detector that has been designed specifically for nugget hunting will have ground balancing features that are designed to mediate this problem.

Why a Gold Specific Detector?

Using a metal detector specifically designed for gold detecting is important when searching for gold nuggets due to a variety of reasons:

- **Sensitivity to Small Targets:** Gold nuggets, especially smaller ones, can be extremely challenging to detect. They often have low conductivity and are buried in mineralized soils. Metal detectors designed for gold prospecting are highly sensitive to small targets and can detect even tiny gold nuggets that might be missed by standard metal detectors. These specialized detectors can pick up the faint signals emitted by small nuggets, increasing the chances of finding them.

- **Enhanced Ground Balance:** Gold prospecting metal detectors have advanced ground balancing capabilities. Mineralized soils that are naturally found in gold-bearing areas can cause false signals and interfere with target detection. Specialized detectors for gold are equipped with features like manual or automatic ground balance adjustments, which help to minimize the impact of ground mineralization noise, making it easier to detect gold nuggets.

- **Higher Frequency Operation:** Gold prospecting metal detectors often operate at higher frequencies compared to general-purpose detectors. Higher frequencies are more effective at detecting small, low-conductivity targets like gold nuggets. They provide better sensitivity to small gold particles and allow the detector to penetrate mineralized soils more effectively.

- **Target Discrimination:** Most gold-specific metal detectors usually offer advanced target discrimination capabilities. They can distinguish between different types of metals and help identify gold targets amidst other metals or trash items. However, while discrimination may be necessary in certain areas, relying too heavily on this feature can result in missed gold. We will discuss this in more detail later in this book.

- **Search Coil Size and Configuration:** Metal detectors designed for gold prospecting often come with a wide-variety of specialized search coils. Many of these coils are often smaller and more maneuverable, allowing prospectors to access narrow or confined spaces where gold nuggets might be located. Other coils are very large, providing added power to detect the deepest nuggets.

Until fairly recently, the best nugget hunting detectors were gold-specific, meaning that they were specifically designed for the purpose of finding gold nuggets, but a poor option for detecting coins in a park for example.

There were a few multi-use detectors that were somewhat good at finding gold too, but most serious nugget hunters still didn't use them.

This has changed somewhat in recent years, and now there are a few different detectors on the market that are just as capable in the goldfields as they are in the park looking for coins or relics.

VLF vs. PI vs. ZVT

For the past few decades, there have primarily been two general types of metal detectors; very-low frequency (VLF) and pulse induction (PI). These are different types of detectors each with its own operating principles and characteristics. Of course, a technical book could probably be written about this, but that wouldn't necessarily be useful for the average nugget hunter. Instead I will provide just a very short summary of these technologies, but more importantly, we will talk about the pros and cons of each technology for the gold hunter.

VLF detectors operate by transmitting a low-frequency electromagnetic field into the ground. When the transmitted signal encounters a metal object, it generates an electromagnetic response in the target, which is then detected by the receiver coil of the detector. VLF detectors rely on the phase shift and amplitude change of the received signal to identify and discriminate between different types of metals.

PI detectors work on a different principle. They emit short bursts or pulses of high-frequency magnetic fields into the ground. When the pulse is turned off, the magnetic field collapses, and any metal objects in the vicinity create a secondary magnetic field in response. PI detectors measure the decay time of the secondary magnetic field to identify the presence of a metal target.

More importantly than the technical aspects of these detectors are how they work in the field. There are pros and cons of each type, and the best choice can depend on the location that you are hunting.

VLF detectors are generally more sensitive to smaller and shallow targets. They can effectively detect small objects like coins, jewelry, and relics at shallower depths due to their ability to discriminate between various metals. VLF detectors are commonly used for coin shooting, jewelry hunting, and relic hunting because of their accurate discrimination abilities. They can excel in goldfields where small, shallow gold is present, or in areas where iron trash requires the use of discrimination features to separate out the gold from other targets.

PI detectors generally have limited target discrimination capabilities. They tend to detect all types of metals without differentiation, making it challenging to discriminate between valuable targets and unwanted objects. This can result in more digging and exploration to confirm the nature of the detected target.

PI detectors are known for their deeper detection capabilities. They can detect larger metal targets, including deeply buried objects and those located in highly mineralized soils.

VLF detectors can be highly affected by mineralization in the ground, which is the presence of minerals and magnetic properties that can create false signals or interfere with target detection. Good VLF detectors will have manual or automatic ground balance controls to help mitigate the effects of mineralization and maintain detection accuracy.

PI detectors have become the preferred type of detector for most nugget shooters because of their ability to handle the highly mineralized soils that are common in most nugget producing areas.

Some of the newer Minelab metal detectors are using a proprietary technology called zero-voltage-transmittion (ZVT). While technically this is different than previous detectors on the market, it functionally acts similar to a PI detector, with similar benefits and drawbacks when compared to a VLF detector.

Cost Considerations

The price range for gold nugget metal detectors can vary depending on the brand, model, features, and technology incorporated. Generally speaking, VLF metal detectors have a lower price point, whereas PI detectors are higher in price.

For new gold nugget detectors, prices for a good basic VLF detector starts at around $500 up to about $1000. In contrast, the newer PI and ZVT detectors on the market start at around $2500 and go up to over $8,000.

Obviously, the high costs for the newest top-of-the-line detector models is going to dissuade a lot of new detectorists. Let me be the first to say that **you do not need to get the latest, greatest high-priced detector models to find gold nuggets!** There are many more reasonable options that you can find that will get you started finding gold. Don't get discouraged just because you don't have $8,000+ dollars to spend on a metal detector.

Below we will discuss some of the most popular gold detectors on the market. Undoubtedly new models will come onto the market after this book is published, but the list below is a good starting point for your research.

If price point is an issue for you, there are many older detectors models that can still be commonly found used (eBay, Craigslist, Facebook Marketplace, etc.) for just a few hundred dollars that are still very good nugget detectors. Most metal detectors are very reliable, and good used detectors can provide many years of service if well cared for.

Popular Brands of Gold Detectors

Here is a list of quality gold nugget detectors that have been produced in the past 20 years or so. Some of these are no longer being sold new, but they are still quality detectors that you may be able to find used at a great price.

I am including some basic notes about these detectors, but I want to avoid filling this section with redundant content that reads like a user manual. I will highlight a few of my favorites, and I encourage you to do additional research on any of these detectors. There are many internet websites and forums that discuss these specific detector models in greater detail.

VLF detectors

Fisher Gold Bug Pro

The Fisher Gold Bug Pro is a popular entry-level gold prospecting metal detector known for its sensitivity to small gold nuggets. It operates at 19 kHz, and while not as sensitive as some other gold detectors on the market, it is very user friendly and operates well in mineralized soils, especially for a VLF detector. With its affordable price point, it offers good performance and is suitable for beginner gold hunters.

In terms of all-around ease of use, the Gold Bug Pro is hard to beat. A very simple, functional gold detector at a reasonable price.

Fisher Gold Bug 2

The Fisher Gold Bug 2 was released in 1995, and for many years it was widely regarded as the best metal detector for small gold. It operates at 71 kHz and can find even tiny specks of gold under the right conditions. Even 25+ years later, there are many nugget shooters that still use the Gold Bug 2 with great success.

White's GMT

White's Electronics was one of the oldest and most popular names in metal detecting, but the company went out of business in 2020. The White's GMT operates at 48 kHz and remains a highly capable gold detector. As of the time of this writing this detector can still be purchased new online. However, with the company no longer operating, the availability to find parts and future repairs might be come an issue that is worth your consideration.

Tesoro Lobo SuperTraq

Tesoro is another detector company that has gone out of business in recent years. Their Tosoro Lobo SuperTraq was their best gold nugget detector running at 17.8 kHz and it worked quite well on small gold. This is another detector that you might be able to find used for a very good price now.

Whites Goldmaster 24k

The Whites Goldmaster 24k features a 48 kHz operating frequency, which provides excellent sensitivity to small gold nuggets and fine gold jewelry. With its automatic ground balancing capabilities and adjustable sensitivity, the Goldmaster 24k can handle mineralized soils and challenging detecting conditions. The detector offers various search modes, including All Metal, Discrimination, and Iron Discrimination, allowing users to customize their detecting experience. It has a lightweight and ergonomic design with a large

LCD screen and intuitive controls.

Nokta Makro Gold Kruzer

The Gold Kruzer is a highly sensitive detector that does an excellent job on small gold. It also has a good entry-level price that makes it a good choice for beginners. It operates at 61 kHz, excellent discrimination features and is fully submersible up to 5 meters. Online firmware updates allow users to get the most out of their detector.

Minelab Equinox 800

This is my current favorite VLF detector right now, and the one that I personally uses when hunting in areas where I need the discrimination features of a VLF. It has 4 modes, making it a truly multi-purpose metal detector, but the gold setting with 40 kHz frequency are how I use it. It is submersible to 3 meters, allows for custom search profiles that can be saved to your preferences, wireless audio and a modern user interface. The Equinox has a lot of features that allow you to dial in the detector to the conditions that you are hunting.

Minelab Gold Monster 1000

The Gold Monster is another fantastic offering from Minelab, and probably their most popular VLF for gold detecting at the moment. It is a very simple "turn on and go" machine, which many users prefer. It has a waterproof coil and excellent discrimination. Regarding their ability to find small gold nuggets at shallow depths, I find the Equinox 800 and the Gold Monster 1000 to be very similar. The main difference is ease of use... if you prefer a simpler machine then the Gold Monster is for you. If you like the ability to adjust setting as well as use it for coins/relics, then go with the Equinox.

XP Deus

When the XP Deus was released in 2009 it was a very popular detector that introduced many new features not yet seen on metal detectors like wireless headphones. Different search coil options could be used to change the frequency of the detector. This detector is a highly capable gold detector, but the Minelab detectors above have most of the same features at a better price which makes them a more popular choice with most gold hunters today.

PI Detectors

White's TDI

The White's TDI was their first PI gold machine. It is a decent detector, but probably my least favorite off all listed in this section. They are also out of production, but are fairly common to find them used. If you are looking for an economical way to get a used PI detector then this might be a good inexpensive option for you.

Garrett ATX

The Garrett ATX is a quality PI detector and very capable in the goldfields. It is fairly simple to use and operate, with several coil options that offer good sensitivity to gold at decent depths. The current price puts it on the lower end of the Pulse Induction detectors currently on the market. The biggest drawback with the ATX is that it is heavy and awkward. The body of the detector is thick and clunky, which may be a problem for many users.

Minelab SDC 2300

The SDC 2300 is a unique PI detector that is fits an interesting niche in the detecting arsenal. It's design allows it to be folded up onto a compact unit, perfect for packing in to remote areas or scrambling through dense underbrush. It is also waterproof to 3 meters allowing for underwater searching. The SDC 2300 does have some coil limitations though... with only a few aftermarket coils to choose from. The design is also a bit awkward and cumbersome, which is the trade-off for how compact and portable it is.

Minelab GPX Series

The earliest Pulse Induction detectors from Minelab (SD2000, 2100, 2200) came out in the mid-1990s and revolutionized gold detecting. They were followed by the GP series (3000, 3500). You might still find these used, and they are still great detectors. In more recent years it has been the GPX series. The 4000, 4500, 5000 are excellent detectors. Most will agree that the later models have a slight edge on small and deep gold, although the improvements over the decades have been incremental. Now the GPX 6000 is the latest offering from Minelab, and a new favorite among serious gold hunters. It has extreme sensitivity to small gold, and can detect those nuggets at depths that are quite impressive. The price of this detector is high, so it won't be the best choice for everyone, but if you're looking for the best, this will be one to consider.

A nice little nugget found with a GPX-4500 while hunting in Northern Nevada.

Garrett Axiom

The Axiom is the latest PI detector from Garrett, and offers the most features and best nugget detecting capabilities. This detector has all the features that prospectors have come to expect from new PI machines, and offers it at a price point several thousand dollars below the latest detectors from Minelab. At just 4.5 pounds, it weighs significantly less than some others. I know several gold detectorists who have been loyal to Minelab for decades that traded in their GPX series machines for the Axiom. That's saying a lot.

ZVT detectors

Minelab GPZ 7000

The GPZ 7000 would probably be considered the "Cadillac" of all gold detectors currently on the market, unfortunately with a price to match. It handles mineralized soils well, punches deep on gold nuggets, and ability to detect small nuggets at shallow to medium depth is impressive. Many gold hunters consider this to be the best on the market, and it is true that the capabilities are impressive. It is a heavy detector, which may detract some users. Personally, I find that the capabilities of the GPX 6000 and the Garrett Axiom are right inline with what the GPZ 7000 offers at a much more affordable price.

Important Note: Long-Range Detectors

While reading and doing researching on various types of metal detectors, you will undoubtedly come across advertisements for so-called "Long Range Detectors." They will make wild claims about being able to locate gold and precious metals at extreme depths and distances, sometimes as far as miles away or hundreds of feet deep. These "detectors" usually look like a ray gun similar to something you might have seen on The Jetsons.

I could go into great detail on these, but to keep it short and concise, I will say that in my experience these so-called "detectors" are no more than scams. They may look and sound fancy and sophisticated, but in reality they are designed to fool uneducated people. I recommend you avoid them if you value your money. I know many experienced nugget shooters who will gladly spend thousands of dollars to use the best-of-the-best equipment available to them. NONE of them use this kind of detector.

Nugget Hunting Accessories

The metal detector is your most important tool, but there are also a wide array of tools and equipment that you want to carry with you while you are out searching the goldfields. The detector might be able to find a target, but you'll be out of luck if you don't have a way to dig it up.

Here are a few accessories that you will want to add to your arsenal.

Digging Pick

A good quality pick is a must-have tool. Gold nuggets can be found in various types of soil and terrain, including rocky areas. A sturdy digging pick made from high-quality materials such as hardened steel or reinforced alloys can withstand the rigors of digging in tough ground conditions without bending or breaking. A pick helps you dig through hard-packed dirt, rocky soils, and dense material, making your digging process faster and more effective.

In many areas, you can expect to spend more time digging than you will detecting, so a good quality pick is a must.

Choose a pick that suits the hunting conditions of the area, and one that matches your detector. For example, if you are using a VLF detector in an area known for smaller gold, a smaller pick with a shorter handle will probably be better suited to the hunting conditions.

Another place where a smaller pick can be ideal is when you are hunting in very brush areas. If you have ever hunted in thick manzanita or similar brush that requires you to crawl on your hands and knees, then you know that dragging along a 3-foot long pick isn't any fun.

Conversely, if you are using a PI detector and are frequently digging up targets that are 1-2 feet deep or more, then you will quickly realize that a bigger, heavier pick is the way to go. Digging those deep 2' craters for a deep piece of gold (or iron rubbish) with a short, lightweight pick is an exercise in futility.

I personally use either an 18" pick or a 30" pick depending on the situation. Both picks have a pointed end and a blunt end, with a few strong magnets attached to quickly locate iron targets.

Whichever pick you go with, make sure to attach several strong magnets to the head of the pick. This will speed up the recovery process by picking up any pieces of iron that you may be digging for. Remember, 99% of the targets you dig will be trash, not gold. To be a successful gold hunter, you need to be able to recover those targets as quickly as possible so you can move on to the next target. A strong magnet will pick up ferrous metals quickly so you can keep hunting.

Headphones

Detecting without headphones always seems appealing when the temperatures are hot, but I always go back to using them. They just work better for me when listening to faint signals. Under perfect, quiet conditions I think I could probably find just as much gold without them, but in real world situations I find that they help immensely to cancel out background noise from wind, but also road noise, creeks and rivers, and other distractions.

I don't have a strong preference on brands. I've used cheap sets and I've used expensive ones... they all seem similar to me. Ask around and you'll hear different opinions.

Trash Pouch

Get a simple pouch that you can wear around your waist to put your trash targets in. *Don't just toss them back on the ground after you dig them up!* For one reason, we should be cleaning up the landscape of trash. A more selfish reason would be that we want to remove the target so that we don't have to deal with it again. I have hunted many areas over and over, and I don't want to keep finding the same target. Pack out trash!

You can pick up a simple tool pouch or tool "apron" from your local hardware store that will do the job just fine.

Nugget Scoop

A pick is best for digging deep holes, but once you get close to the target a nugget scoop is the best tool for finding your nugget.

A nugget scoop is designed to be gentle on fragile targets, such as delicate gold nuggets or small specimens. The scoop's design, which typically includes smooth edges and non-abrasive materials, helps prevent damage to the targets during retrieval. This is particularly important when dealing with valuable and easily damaged gold nuggets.

A good scoop should be made from a high-impact plastic so that it won't set off your detector. This allows you to sweep dirt over the coil and listen for a gold nugget inside the scoop.

Using a nugget scoop when metal detecting for gold nuggets improves target recovery, increases efficiency, and protects fragile targets from damage.

Gold Bottle

You'll need a good bottle to hold any gold nuggets that you find. I like the orange plastic match holders that you can find at Army/Navy stores. They are a good size to fit comfortably in your pocket while being large enough to hold most nuggets.

Test Nugget

This is optional, but many detectorists like to bring a gold nugget out with them into the field. It is used when you first set up your detector to "tune your ear" to the sound of gold, and to adjust the settings of your detector for optimal use.

Choose the smallest nugget that your detector can hear. As one old prospector once told me, "The big nuggets find themselves," meaning that their metal detector will surely sound off loudly on a bigger nugget. It's the small ones that you've got to listen for.

Since it can be easy to lose a small nugget, it's not a bad idea to glue your test nugget to something larger like a guitar pick. Toss it on the ground to tune your detector with, then put it back safely in your pocket for the rest of the day.

Handheld Pinpointer

Using a handheld pinpointer when metal detecting provides several advantages. It allows for more precise and targeted recovery of detected objects, especially in situations where the target may be small, buried deep, or hidden within a larger area of soil or debris.

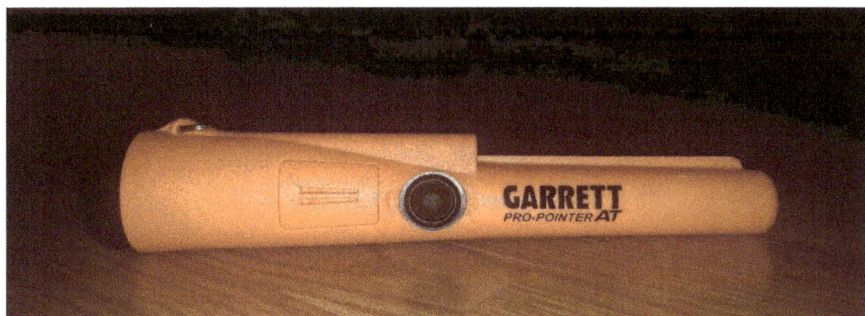

By narrowing down the search area, the pinpointer saves time and effort, minimizing unnecessary digging and reducing the chances of damaging valuable targets. Its compact and portable design makes it easy to carry.

I don't carry one if I am using a VLF detector with a smaller coil size, but they can be especially helpful when you are digging deep targets with a larger search coil. A good pinpointer can save you a lot of time.

Coil Selection

Having a variety of different search coils for your metal detector is important because it allows you to adapt to different detecting conditions and target types. Different search coils have varying sizes, shapes, and configurations, which affect their sensitivity, depth capabilities, and target discrimination.

A large coil can cover a larger area and reach greater depths, making it ideal for open fields or searching for deeply buried objects. Conversely, a smaller search coil offers increased sensitivity and maneuverability, making it suitable for trashy or congested areas where target separation is crucial.

Specialized coils for Pulse Induction metal detectors, such as concentric or DD coils, Can provide enhanced performance in specific environments or for specific targets. Generally you will find that concentric coils give you better depth, but in some highly mineralized soils a DD coil may operate more smoothly and actually give you better results. They can also be advantageous near power lines.

Some detector models have lots of different interchangeable coil options to choose from. I've tried dozens of different coils over the years, but nowadays I find that simple is better. A medium sized, elliptical mono coil suits my needs for the majority of my hunting situations.

Extra Batteries

This should be a no-brainer, but carrying extra batteries is always a good idea. You don't want to be a long way from your truck only to have your battery die. Bring at least one extra set of fully-charged detector batteries with you on your hunts, and keep a charger at camp so you can top them off when you get back in the evening.

Extra Clothing

Dress in layers and do your best to prepare for the worst scenario. I was once on a detecting trip in Northern Nevada. It was June, and the temperatures were in the 80s. Throughout the day, a storm came blowing in and the temperatures dropped down into the 40s. With that stiff breeze, I expect the wind chill factor made it well below freezing.

I had only a very light jacket with me, and to put it simply I was unprepared. I tried my best to power through it, but it was just too cold to focus on metal detecting. I went back to camp and lost out on that day of detecting.

Non-Metallic Boots

Using non-metallic footwear is of utmost importance when metal detecting due to their ability to minimize interference and maintain the accuracy of metal detectors. When wearing boots with metal eyelets, this will result in false signals that can get frustrating.

Tennis shoes will work, but they don't provide the best protection or functionality in general.

Non-metallic boots will give you the best of both worlds. They will prevent interference by reducing the presence of metal in close proximity to the detector's coil.

Sunscreen

Sunscreen is essential for outdoor activities as it helps protect the skin from harmful ultraviolet (UV) rays emitted by the sun. Regular use of sunscreen reduces the risk of sunburn, skin damage, premature aging, and the development of skin cancer, emphasizing its crucial role in maintaining skin health and safety while enjoying the outdoors.

Food/Water

Always carry more food and water with you than you think you will need. You may expect that you'll be staying close to camp or near your vehicle, but plans have a way of changing when you are out in the field.

If I am hunting in the summer and expect temperatures to get hot by afternoon, I will freeze a couple water bottles so that they are solid ice. By late afternoon the ice will thaw and you will still have nice cold water.

Bring compact dense items like nuts, granola bars, and other caloric foods. These will give you plenty of calories while still being compact and lightweight.

Maps

In my opinion, you should always carry a paper map with you when you are outdoors. People today have become very reliant on GPS unit and handheld phones. These work great most of the time, but a dead battery or a slip into a creek might make them inoperable. Carry a map with you and learn how to read it.

Backpack

A good backpack is necessary to carry all your supplies for the day. You want it to be lightweight enough that it isn't too cumbersome while you are detecting, but it needs to be large enough to carry all of your supplies.

Safety in the Goldfields

Many of the best prospecting areas throughout the US and the world are well off the beaten path. You will often find yourself in areas far from civilization, on dirt roads and away from services. You need to be prepared to handle problems that may arise by yourself.

Carrying supplies in your vehicle when venturing out into the backcountry is crucial for preparedness and safety. In case of unexpected situations or emergencies, having essential supplies can provide you with the means to address basic needs, perform minor repairs, or wait for assistance. These supplies help mitigate risks, increase self-reliance, and enhance your ability to handle unforeseen circumstances, ensuring a safer and more secure backcountry experience.

Vehicle Choice

First and foremost, your vehicle needs to capable of handling the roads in area that you intend to prospect. In some areas a car may be just fine, but if you intend to go very far off-road, I recommend a 4x4 pickup with good clearance.

The rugged terrains and challenging conditions encountered in off-road environments demand a vehicle that is up to the task. A vehicles ability to engage all four wheels provides enhanced traction, allowing it to navigate through mud, snow, sand, and uneven surfaces with greater ease. This increased traction minimizes the risk of getting stuck or losing control, ensuring a safer and more successful off-road adventure.

Additionally, the higher ground clearance and durable suspension systems found in 4x4 vehicles enable them to traverse obstacles such as rocks, fallen branches, and steep inclines, expanding the possibilities for exploration. You can expect to encounter all of these things and more when you venture out into the goldfields.

Using an ATV (All-Terrain Vehicle) or UTV (Utility Task Vehicle) for off-road travel can also offer numerous benefit. These versatile vehicles are specifically designed to excel in rugged environments, providing exceptional maneuverability, agility, and versatility. With their lightweight and compact design, they can navigate narrow trails and tight spaces that larger vehicles may struggle with.

A major benefit is also that they boast excellent suspension systems that allow for smooth rides over rough terrain. The ability to carry equipment and supplies in dedicated cargo spaces also makes them ideal for outdoor adventures, work purposes, or recreational activities.

Everyone's situation (and budget) is different, but regardless of what you choose to drive to navigate out to gold country, make sure that it is capable of handling the situation.

Shelter

Obviously, you will need some sort of shelter when you are away from home. For many years, I did just fine prospected out of a basic tent. As I've gotten older, I've learned to appreciate a comfortable bed at night, so I've upgraded to a small camper trailer. I know prospectors older than me who sleep in the bed of their pickup. Whatever works for you is fine, as long as it protects you from the elements.

Fueling up in Searchlight, Nevada on my way to go prospecting for a few weeks in Northern Arizona. This simple setup has treated me well over the years.

Food

When embarking on a multi-day trip into the backcountry, you want to bring all the food you expect to need and a little bit more. It's always better to have too much than it is to have not enough.

I generally set up a base camp that I leave from every morning and return to in the evening. I will eat a meal at camp in the morning, then load up my pack with snacks and lunch, then have dinner when I return to camp that evening.

It's important to load your day pack with lightweight and non-perishable foods that provide sustained energy. Some good options include trail mix, energy bars, dehydrated meals, jerky, nut butter, crackers or rice cakes, dried fruit, hard cheeses, and instant oatmeal. These foods are easy to carry, require minimal preparation, and offer a good balance of carbohydrates, protein, and healthy fats.

Considering any dietary restrictions or personal preferences, these choices will keep you nourished and energized throughout your prospecting adventure.

Tool Kit

Anytime you are traveling in areas with limited services, it's important to be prepared for potential challenges or emergencies. You should always carry some basic tools that you keep with you in your truck. If you are using an ATV or UTV, you should carry an appropriate tool kit there as well. Here are a few things to consider.

1. Tire repair kit: Include a tire plug kit or a patch kit to fix punctures quickly. Additionally, an air compressor can help reinflate tires after repair or adjust tire pressure for different terrains.
2. Recovery straps and shackles: These sturdy straps and heavy-duty shackles are essential for vehicle recovery, such as towing or winching. Opt for straps with a high tensile strength and proper load rating.
3. Hi-lift jack: A versatile tool for lifting your vehicle, the hi-lift jack can assist in changing tires, vehicle recovery, and creating additional ground clearance. These can be dangerous, so be sure you have proper instruction and training before operating a hi-lift.
4. Shovel: A sturdy shovel can come in handy for digging out stuck tires. They are also a must-have tool in general to have with you at camp.
5. Gloves: Protect your hands during repairs or recovery operations with a durable pair of work gloves. Most of you will likely be using gloves already while prospecting.
6. Basic tool kit: Carry a set of essential tools, including wrenches, pliers, screwdrivers, socket set, and Allen keys. These can help you handle minor repairs or adjustments while out in the field.

7. Duct tape and zip ties: These versatile items can provide temporary fixes for a wide variety of issues you may encounter.

8. Jumper cables or portable jump starter: In case of a dead battery, jumper cables or a portable jump starter can get you back on the road quickly.

9. Fire extinguisher: Carry a compact fire extinguisher suitable for extinguishing small fires. Make sure it is appropriately rated for automotive use.

10. First aid kit: Accidents can happen anywhere, so have a well-stocked first aid kit on hand to address minor injuries.

11. Flashlight or headlamp: A reliable light source is crucial, especially during nighttime repairs or emergency situations. Have extra batteries too.

12. Spare fluids: Carry spare engine oil, coolant, and any other necessary fluids specific to your vehicle.

13. Portable air compressor: Useful for maintaining proper tire pressure or inflating air mattresses and other equipment.

14. Tire pressure gauge: Monitor tire pressure accurately and adjust it according to the terrain requirements.

15. Maps, compass, and GPS: Keep a physical map of the area, a compass for navigation, and a reliable GPS device or smartphone app.

Remember, these are general suggestions, and the specific tools you carry may vary depending on your vehicle, the terrain, and the length of your off-road trips. It's also important to have proper training and knowledge to use these tools effectively and safely.

Water

Above all else, **water is the single most important thing to have with you at all times when venturing out into gold country.** If you get lost, it isn't the bears or the mountain lions that will kill you... most people that get lost in the backcountry die from dehydration.

Carrying an ample supply of water is crucial for maintaining hydration, preventing dehydration-related symptoms and heat-related illnesses, sustaining physical performance and endurance, regulating body temperature, and providing a vital resource for emergencies or unexpected situations, ensuring safety, well-being, and preparedness.

People have a tendency to get careless because they don't think of the worst case scenarios. I can't tell you how many times I have been hiking or camping with someone, and they wouldn't bother to pack any water, or perhaps just one small bottle.

- "Oh, it's not going to get very hot today."
- "We're only going a mile, I'll be fine."
- "If I get thirst I'll just drink from a stream."

These are all incredibly dangerous mindsets that can get you killed. Carry lots of water, more than you think you will need. If you are in an area that you know for certain will have a water source nearby, then it's okay to bring one bottle and a good water purifier with you, but I would still carry at least a gallon of water in your pack.

Back at camp, the amount you need will depend on how many days you will be camping and how far away a source is. At a minimum, I would get a good portable water container that carries about 5-gallons. But again, every situation is different. If you are going to be spending a week in remote Northern Nevada and there are few water sources, then you might need 20 gallons or more. Play it safe. **Carry more than you need.**

Cell Phone/Satellite Phone/Spot Unit

Cell phone coverage has gotten much better in recent years, and many areas have reliable coverage even many miles outside of the city.

Some people carry a satellite phone or some type of location-based GPS device with them out in the field. Many years ago these were incredibly expensive and cost-prohibitive for the average prospector, but in recent years they have gotten quite affordable, making them an excellent consideration if you venture deep into the backcountry.

These devices can offer a peace of mind, but you should never depend on them. Just because you have a cell phone in your pocket in case of emergency, it's is no excuse to go unprepared. Make sure you've got food, water and shelter covered.

Tell others Where You are Going

Informing others about your intended destination when you are venturing into the backcountry is of utmost importance for your safety. By sharing your plans with trusted individuals, you provide them with crucial information that can aid in rescue and emergency response efforts if needed.

If you're ever alone and find yourself in need of emergency assistance, you will be glad that you told a friend or family member where you were going.

In the event of an accident, injury, or unexpected delay, those who know your whereabouts can alert authorities, initiate a search, or provide assistance. This simple act of communication enhances your chances of being found promptly, especially in remote areas with limited cell phone reception.

Stay out of Old Mines!

Staying out of old abandoned underground mines is of paramount importance due to countless hazards associated with these sites. I know that we are out here looking for gold, so it seems like the best place to look would be around these old mines where the old timers were looking.

Yes, prospecting *around and adjacent to old mines* is indeed a great way to find gold, but I would advise you to never go underground. Stay on the surface and use extreme caution anytime you are around these old mining sites.

Abandoned mines lack maintenance and regular safety inspections, making them structurally unsound and prone to collapse, posing a severe risk to anyone entering. Many of the mines you will find in the United States are well over 100 years old. Their support structures are rotted out and the chances of a cave-in are extremely high.

There are thousands of abandoned mines throughout the West. The Bureau of Land Management has undergone extensive efforts to seal off many of these open shafts, but there are still thousands that of undocumented sites that present a real danger to the public. Use extreme caution while exploring around old mines.

Secondly, mines can contain toxic gases, such as carbon monoxide, methane, or hydrogen sulfide, which can accumulate in enclosed spaces and lead to asphyxiation or poisoning. Additionally, abandoned mines may have unstable or hazardous materials, including chemicals, asbestos, or heavy metals, which can contaminate the air or water sources, causing serious health problems if exposed.

Top States for Gold Nuggets

You Can't Find Gold Nuggets where they Don't Exist!

This is one of the most important things you should take away from this book. Where you spend your time metal detecting for gold nuggets is more important than any single other factor. You can't find gold nuggets where they don't exist!

A prospector using an inferior quality metal detector in an area where gold nuggets are likely to occur still has a *chance* of finding a piece of gold. The opposite is not true! You can have the best, most expensive gold detector in the world, but if you are searching in an area where gold nuggets simply don't exist then you are going to go home empty-handed.

Because of this, the best piece of advice I give to new gold prospectors is to search in areas where gold has been found before. This is true of you are panning, sluicing, or any other method, but it's especially important if you are using a metal detector. Not only do you need to find areas where gold occurs, but you need areas where gold nugget occur.

Gold deposits are typically found in specific geological formations or areas with favorable conditions for gold mineralization. These areas may contain gold-bearing veins, placers (deposits of eroded gold), or other geological formations that have concentrated gold over time. By focusing on known gold-bearing areas, you increase your chances of finding gold nuggets.

A history of gold mining or prospecting is another excellent indicator. These areas were likely explored extensively by early miners who had firsthand knowledge of gold-rich locations. Their knowledge and experience can serve as valuable clues for modern-day prospectors. Searching in these areas gives you a head start by targeting locations that have already demonstrated gold potential.

Spending time to research areas of past mining activity and learn how to identify locations that have the potential to produce detectable gold nuggets is critical to your success. This is an important distinction because there are many, many rich gold prospecting areas that only produce fine gold, and almost never produce nuggets. We will more about all of this in future chapters, but first I want to provide a short overview of states that produce gold nuggets.

About 20 of the 50 states in the US have areas where gold nuggets can be found. Some of these rich gold-bearing areas are quite extensive, while other states such have only a few limited areas where gold has occurred in the form of nuggets large enough to be found with a metal detector.

This section provides basic information on some known nugget producing locations throughout the United States. Not all of the nuggets shown here were found with a metal detector, but their existence is proof that large nuggets have been found, and still hold potential for the modern-day prospector.

Please know that there are entire books written about gold mining in some of these states, so the information you will find here is certainly not complete. Consider this a brief introduction to compel you to doing further research on these areas that you might want to explore.

Alaska

Alaska has historically been one of the largest gold producers in the United States, and it still ranks as one of the top gold mining states. Over half of the total gold production can be credited to two major gold regions; Nome and the Klondike. (The Klondike is actually just over the boundary in the Yukon, but most historical data credited the gold to Alaska.) There are dozens of major and minor gold districts across the state, and many of have historically produced very large gold nuggets.

A handful of chunky nuggets found near Fairbanks.

With such a rich gold mining history, many will be surprised when I tell them that Alaska is actually a very challenging place to go gold prospecting, and even more challenging place to metal detect for gold.

The main reason for this is access. Alaska is a massive state. And although it has produced tons of gold over the past century, there are also vast areas that are not suitable for gold detecting. Just like anywhere else, only a very tiny percentage of the landscape has any detectable gold. And those areas that do have detectable gold are heavily claimed by large mining operations and not accessible for most prospectors. Research is just as important here as anywhere else.

There are many rich gold areas on the Seward Peninsula. The best known are the famous beach placers of Nome. While most of the gold found in the sand at Nome is fine textured, nearby Anvil Creek just west of town has produced some massive gold nuggets over the years! A nugget weighing 182 troy ounces was found here, and it was the largest nugget found in Alaska for nearly a century. There have been several documented discoveries of nuggets in Anvil Creek that weighed over 100 ounces. It still holds great potential for large nuggets.

There are also many rich mining districts a few hundred miles southeast of the Seward Peninsula along the Yukon and Kuskokwim Rivers. The Kuskokswim Gold Belt is described as a broken belt of gold bearing rocks that have the reputation of producing large nuggets and considerable gold.

LARGEST NUGGETS EVER FOUND IN ALASKA
OWNED BY PIONEER MINING Co. FROM ANVIL CREEK NOME.
Copyright 1904 By F. H. NOWELL.

Three nuggets found at Anvil Creek ranging from 97 to 182 troy ounces!

Some of the better known mining districts in this belt are the Fortymile and Iditarod districts. Two areas in this region that are well-known for producing large gold nuggets are Ganes Creek and Moore Creek, both of which have been popular destinations for gold prospectors using metal detectors.

Chicken Creek is another gold rich destination in this area where gold was discovered way back in 1896. Gold panning and placer mining is popular around Chicken. Recreational miners have reported finding multi-ounce nuggets in this area with nice nuggets continuing to be found.

Jack Wade Creek Gold Panning Area runs along the Taylor Highway just a few miles north of Chicken. There are several miles of creek that are unclaimed and open to panning, sluicing and metal detecting. This is another area that can produce some really nice nuggets if you put in the time. Running a good metal detector over the old tailing piles can be very productive.

Further inland, many gold bearing areas are found on the Yukon traveling upriver toward the Klondike. Rich placers are found around Fairbanks in the Yukon and Tanana River basins and on the Chena River. The gold discoveries near Fairbanks were discovered as late as 1902, and are considered to be the last great gold rush in America.

Plenty of gold has been found in the area around Cook Inlet in South-central Alaska. The Kenai Peninsula, Cache Creek, Willow Creek, and Valdez Creek are some of major gold districts around Cook Inlet and Anchorage. A lot of big nuggets have been found here too.

The Ruby district is another place where huge gold nuggets are found. The biggest is the Alaska Centennial Nugget. It was found in Swift Creek near the town of Ruby, Alaska in 1998 and weighed a massive 294 troy ounces!

Several of Alaska's largest gold nuggets have come from the Brooks Mountain Range in northern Alaska. Many nuggets have been found near the town of Wiseman that weighed over 100 troy ounces. The Middle Fork of the Koyukuk River, Hammond River, Wiseman Creek, and Nolan Creek all produced some awesome gold, and miners are still finding some impressive gold nuggets here.

Arizona

Arizona is one of the most popular states for gold nugget detecting. It has an exceptional mining history, with many mining districts scattered throughout the entire state. The mild winter climate also attracts a lot of prospectors from all around the country to search for gold during those winter months.

Arizona is also ideal for gold detecting because the geological conditions are well suited for metal detecting in many locations. The vegetation is sparse and the bedrock is often shallow, creating a good environment for detecting.

The Lynx Creek District near Prescott is one of the richest areas of the state and a very popular area with prospectors today. It has been prospected hard over the years, but gold is still be found. The majority of gold recovered from this area has been fine placer deposits from the creek, but searching the many dry gulches that feed into Lynx Creek can be productive for metal detecting.

Groom Creek was another productive drainage. Any of the area directly surrounding Prescott is worth exploring with your metal detector. The Bradshaw Mountains have been a very productive mining region for centuries and the lack of water has always been a challenge for the early miners, meaning they left behind a lot of gold.

The Weaver/Rich Hill District has been one of the major producers in Arizona. Placers can be found at Weaver and Antelope Creeks. This is a popular location among gold detectorists, as it has a known history of producing some very large nuggets. Covering over 40 square miles in size, the area was discovered in the 1860s and had produced gold worth more than a million dollars by the 1880s. The summit of Rich Hill, its gulches and the surrounding areas have been remarkably productive. One location known as the "Potato Patch" was said to have produced countless potato-sized gold nuggets when miners first discovered it at Rich Hill.

The Little San Domingo placers are near Wickenburg. The gold is widespread over a large area and there are lots of little dry washes to explore. There are stories of old-timers picking up big nuggets right on the surface when they first started mining this area. Detectorists have hunted the area hard over the years but there are still nuggets to find. Big ones are still found occasionally, but there is a lot of small gold too. A sensitive gold detector will be important here.

The Gold Basin District is located 50 miles north of Kingman. Much of the historic gold production comes from lode deposits, but there are also a lot of gold nuggets found throughout Gold Basin. Mining started in this district in the early 1870s, covering the eastern part of the White Hills and stretching all the way to Hualapai Wash. The gold deposits here are widely scattered. Any of the dry washes and gulleys have potential to produce nice gold. This area has been detected hard over the years, but the desert is vast and good gold can still be found here with some hard work. I've seen multi-ounce nuggets that were found in Gold Basin.

The desert surrounding Quartzsite and Yuma has vast gold deposits, and many prospectors converge on the area in the winter when temperatures are mild. Gold is abundant throughout Yuma County and metal detecting can produce nice rough-textured nuggets and specimens. The north end of the Gila Mountains and southern side of the Laguna Mountains have both been mined extensively.

Gold was discovered about 40 miles south of Tucson at a mining camp called Greaterville. This created a small boom that brought in many miners which led to a thriving mining town. Water was always a challenge in this area. Ditches were dug to bring in water and work the placers, but there are still a lot of areas that haven't been thoroughly worked thoroughly. The original Greaterville town site is on private property but there are many desert gulches around that have proved to be quite rich for gold prospecting.

We've truly just scratched the surface here. If you are looking for places to go metal detecting for gold in Arizona, I recommend getting a copy of Placer Gold Deposits of Arizona by Maureen Johnson. It covers many of the gold districts across Arizona. You can even find free PDF versions of this old report online.

Washington

Washington is a decent state for gold prospecting, but most areas produce fine gold that is more suitable for panning and sluicing than for metal detecting. There are a handful of mining districts that have produced some nice nuggets which we will discuss.

The most famous gold mining district in Washington is definitely Liberty, a small town about 20 miles north of Ellensburg. It is surrounded by the Okanogan-Wenatchee National Forest.

The thing that makes the area around Liberty so noteworthy is not just the rich mining history, but also that the largest gold nuggets found in Washington have been mined here. Individual nuggets weighing up to 70 ounces have been unearthed from the mines here! This area also produces some fascinating crystalline gold specimens that are highly valued by collectors.

The early arrivals settled near Swauk Creek, and other rich deposits were discovered at nearby Williams Creek. Other places where gold was discovered included Negro Creek, Boulder Creek, and the Baker Creek among others. These creeks have lots of gold, but most of the big nuggets were actually found in ancient river channels up on the surrounding mountains.

An informational kiosk in downtown Liberty shows off visitors some of the incredible crystalline gold specimens that have been found in this mining district. The Rice Museum in Hillsboro, Oregon has one of the largest collections of Liberty gold on display to the public.

South of Liberty is the Cle Elum River placers. There is very good gold in this river and has always been a popular area for dredgers. Many of the tributaries are also gold bearing such as Silver Creek, Fortune Creek, and Big Salmon Creek.

There are several large lode mining districts in Eastern Washington. The town of Republic is a major mining area. The mines of Okanogan County are widespread and very rich. There are numerous mining districts here including the Cascade, Oroville, Nighthawk, Myers Creek, and Methow Mining District. A serious miner should research the many profitable mines that operated here during the late 19th century. These areas aren't necessarily known for nuggets, but there is certainly potential for finding them, and specimens of high-grade gold ore could likely be found in these areas.

The placer deposits scattered throughout the northern Cascade Range are worthy of note, particularly because many of them are not associated with any historic mining camps. There is gold all throughout the creeks and rivers of the Cascades, but you have to go out and find them.

A person willing to backpack into some remote mountains streams has a good chance of finding some nice gold, but a prospector would probably be better armed with a gold pan than with a metal detector. Nuggets can be found in the Cascade Mountains, but they are rare.

Oregon

Oregon is a super place for the prospecting for a couple of reasons. There's a lot of gold there and there is a lot of public land to explore. The northeastern part of the state and the southwestern part of Oregon just above the California border are the two best regions to prospect. Many areas produce nice sized gold nuggets making it a great place to swing a metal detector.

In southwestern Oregon, rich placer deposits were discovered in 1851 in Josephine Creek and some of the other creeks close by. Not long after that gold was discovered at the Rogue, Applegate, and Illinois Rivers.

Gold in lode and placer form is found all through the Siskiyou Mountains. Check out Jackson, Josephine counties along with the south part of Douglas County, as well as some parts of Coos and Curry Counties. Grants Pass and Medford areas are worth a look as they both produced significant amounts of gold in the past.

In Douglas County, check Cow Creek, Myrtle Creek, Last Chance Creek and Quines Creeks, as well as the South Umpqua River and all waters draining into them. There was some hydraulic operations, and both placers and lodes have produced here.

Jackson County is one of Oregon's richest mining areas. This area would be worth your while as over half million ounces have come out of this area since it was discovered in 1852. You can find gold in all the waters here, but definitely explore around Palmer, Sterling, Elk and Willow Creeks. Look for hand stacked rocks and other indicators of past mining activity.

Considerable gold mining took place in Josephine County. Be on the lookout here for old lode mines, placers and hydraulic pits, as plenty of gold came out of this region in the past. Worth checking out are the Illinois River as well as Josephine, Althouse and Galice Creeks. Historical records mention that Althouse Creek may be the source of Oregon's largest gold nuggets, some weighing as much as 17-pounds!

Almost 2/3 of the gold production came from just a few counties in Eastern Oregon. There is a gold belt stretching approximately 100 miles long and 50 miles wide, and it covers much of Union, Grant and Baker Counties. The area is littered with old mines, hydraulic and hand placers, and areas that have been torn up by bucket line dredging. There are lots of nuggets left to find here.

An incredible collection of gold nuggets and specimens from Oregon's Blue Mountains.

This gold belt begins at the Snake River by the Idaho border. Traveling from Huntington to the foot of the Wallowa Mountain range, there are several mining districts that were active in the late 1800s.

The Burnt River flows along Highway 84 and many of the tributaries that flow into it will have gold. Look for ancient gravel deposits situated above the current river channel. Following the river upstream, it eventually splits from the highway and goes west into Burnt River Canyon toward Bridgeport. This area was extensively mined and is worthy of further research. Nearby Clarksville, Malheur City, Eldorado and Rye Valley all have gold.

To the west lie the Blue Mountains, and upstream from Baker the Powder River has been mined since the 1860s. The Sumpter Valley was worked for many years with bucket dredges, and there are miles of stirred up valley floors. Sumpter was a booming mining camp during the height of the gold rush.

Since the older dredges discarded larger pieces by design, the tailing piles still contain nuggets that would have been lost to the miners initially. Some other old mining towns that might be worth checking are Greenhorn, Bourne, Granite and Susanville.

An incredible 80.4 ounce gold nugget was found near the old mining town of Susanville in 1913. If you're ever in Baker City, the nugget is on display at the bank across the street from the Geiser Grand Hotel.

Following the gold belt west, the John Day River and its many forks and drainages are definitely worth a look. Placer gold can be found in most of the creeks in this part of the state. There was considerable mining around John Day and Canyon City. All of these areas not only produced gold, but they produced nice chunky gold that can be found with a metal detector.

California

California is another state that would be impossible to cover in just a few short pages, but we will provide a short summary here to get you started in your research. This is the richest placer mining state in the US, and there are extensive goldfields that cover its entire length. The Sierra Nevada Mountains were the site of the famous "forty-niners" gold rush, and rich gold strikes would eventually be discovered all the way up near the Oregon border down to the Mexico border to the south.

The American River was the first place where gold was discovered in California. In 1948 James Marshall discovered gold on the South Fork of the American River and set off the largest gold rush in American history. Although the easily accessible gold is long gone, the American River is still a great place for a prospecting. One place to check out is the Auburn State Recreation Area the covers parts of the Middle and the North forks of the river. Another excellent location is the Michigan Bluff area on the middle fork. On the South Fork American River, the Marshall Gold Discovery State Historic Park, Mount Murphy Bridge and the area north of Chili Bar are all historically rich mining sites.

The Yuba River is one of the best California's richest rivers to visit if you want to search for gold nuggets. The river was at the heart of the original California gold rush and still produces gold nuggets for the tenacious gold prospectors. One of the best places to prospect for gold on the river is the South Yuba River. In decades past, dredgers found pounds and pounds of gold in the gravels of the Yuba River. Metal detecting is now the best way to find nuggets.

The Feather River was home to hundreds of thousands of miners during the first California gold rush in 1849. Today the river still offers an excellent opportunity to recreational gold miners to prospect and find gold. If you want to find some real goals then you should also consider the small creeks and streams that feed the main river. This small waterways still have rich placers as most prospectors overlook them.

There are hundreds, even thousands of creeks and gulches that feed into these main river drainages throughout the Sierras that contain gold. Many of them are dry year-round, and a metal detector is the best tool to search for gold. This is definitely "nugget country," with some incredible finds being made over the centuries. Most of the largest nuggets found in the US came from California.

Additionally it should be noted that some of the best gold in the Sierras has come from ancient river benches that are situated high above the present river channel. These are ideal locations to search with metal detectors. The same can be said for thousands of lode mines in this region that may have high-grade ore specimens that can be found in waste rock piles and tailings from the mines. We will discuss this hunting technique further in this book.

Far in the most northern part of California is the Klamath River, which was was one of the richest sources of gold during the early days of the Californian gold rush. Gold was discovered on the river and on pretty much all its tributaries and creeks throughout Siskiyou County. One of the richest deposits were on French Gulch and at Yreka.

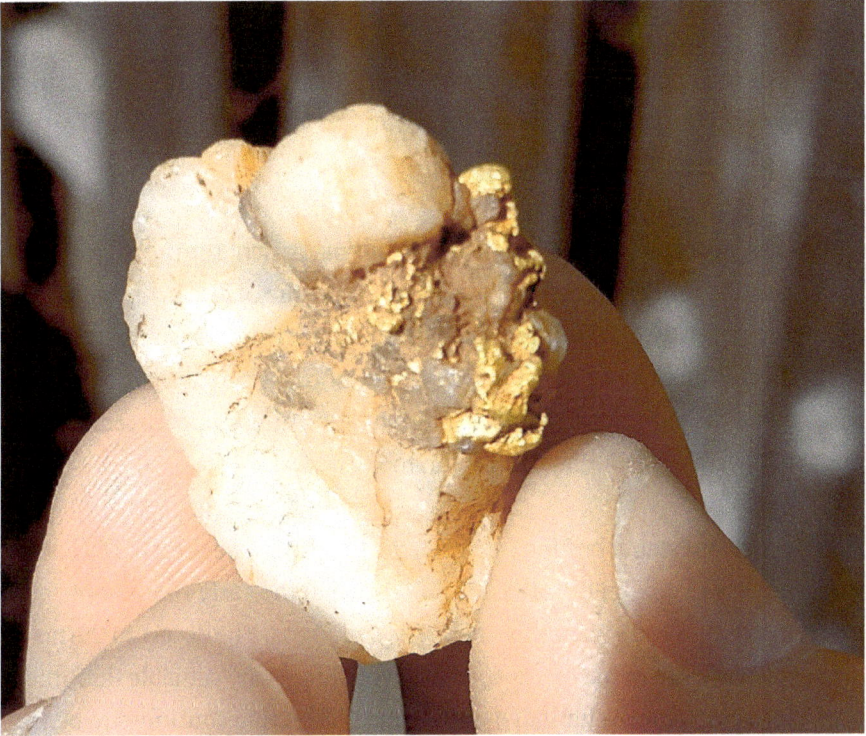

There are many areas in California where high-grade specimens like this can be found by detecting around old tailing piles and the old quartz mines.

The entire Klamath region and many of its tributaries also contain rich gold deposits. Some of the best places to prospect for gold on the Klamath River include Copper Creek, Happy Camp, Scott River, Salmon River, the Trinity River, Clear Creek, and Oak Bar Creek. This is still a great area for prospectors willing to hike into remote areas for a few days.

Weaverville is located in Trinity County, way up in the northernmost section of California. The town is one of the historical gold boom towns in California, but many prospectors overlook the area. Gold was discovered here in 1850. Weaverville is still a good place to look for gold, which can be found in the rivers, creeks and gulches surrounding town. Weaver Creek and its tributaries as well as Trinity River are some of the richest in the basin are rich with gold.

There are many mining towns throughout Siskiyou, Shasta, and Trinity Counties with a rich history of gold mining. Metal detecting can be very productive here.

Northern California gets so much attention for its rich mining history that many people don't realize that southern California also has an incredible mining history as well. The desert region spanning from the southern flanks of the Sierras all the way down to the Mexico border have numerous mining areas that a detectorist can explore. More importantly, some incredible gold nuggets have been found in this region too.

Randsburg was established in 1895 when the Rand Mine was created following the discovery of gold in the area. Mining ended in the early 1900s abut some of the lode mines were opened in the 1980s and 1990s. The desert to the north of the town is quite rich with prospectors recording many valuable finds there over the years. Water is limited here but metal detecting continues to be very productive for nugget hunters. More than half of the gold in Kern County was produced in this area and Yellow Aster Mine accounted for most of it.

The Kern River at Keyesville and Kernville, and north of Lake Isabella that flows through the Sequoia National Forest is another rich mining area. Greenhorn Creek is the site of the first gold discovery near the river. Many prospectors report finding decent-sized gold nuggets here.

The San Gabriel River just outside of Los Angeles produced a significant amount of gold during the early years. Gold was first discovered on the San Gabriel River in 1855. The mining boom on the river ended in the 1930s and since then small-scale mining has been ongoing along the river. One thing to note is that the much of the richest area of the East Fork San Gabriel River is now off-limits to mineral exploration due to recent National Monument designations.

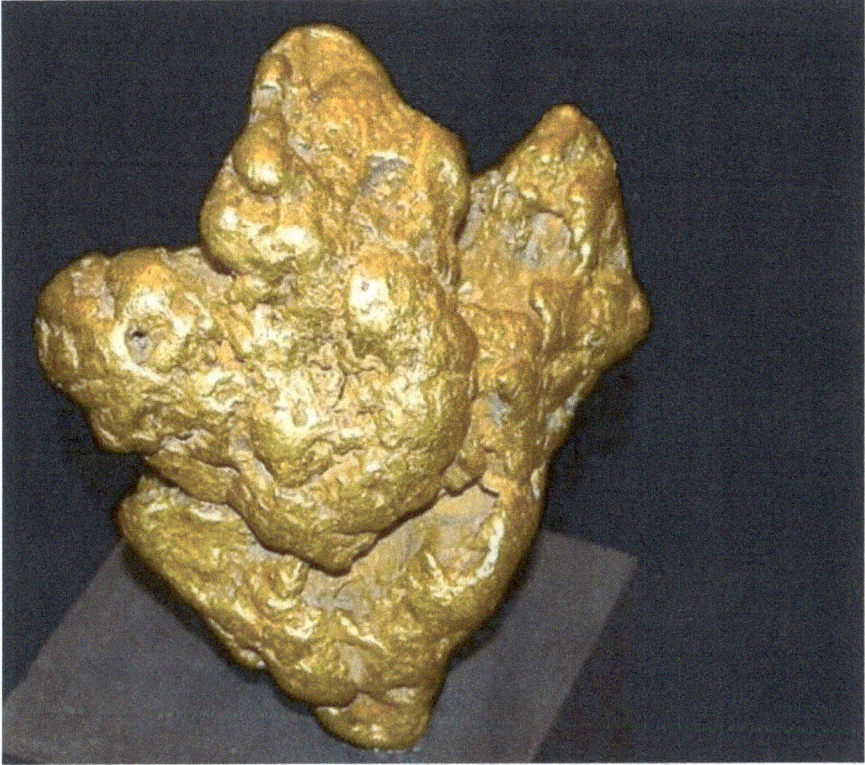

The "Mojave Nugget" is a huge 156-ounce nugget discovered by Ty Paulsen in 1977. He found it using a metal detector in the desert near Randsburg, California. The nugget is now part of the Natural History Museum of Los Angeles.

The Dale Mining district was established in 1881 when gold was discovered in the area. It covers parts of San Bernardino and Riverside Counties, and is located about 18 miles east of Twentynine Palms. Several gold mines were established in the area with the two most productive mines being the Supply Mine and the OK mine. Other notable mines are Carlyle and Gold Crown. Mining continued in the area until the Second World War when the last remaining mines were closed down. Today the district is popular with gold prospectors who use dry washing and metal detecting to find gold. The region has gold close to the surface and this makes it easy for miners to recover as much gold as possible. Most of the mine areas are outside the Joshua Tree National Park and can be accessed using a 4WD vehicle with high clearance.

There are many good resources to help you research mining areas in California. One of the best is a book titled Gold Districts of California by William B. Clark. It was published by the California Division of Mines and Geology, and a PDF version can be found for free online.

Nevada

Nevada is the top gold producing state in the nation. Although gold was first discovered near Gold Canyon, close to Virginia City, it was the later discovery in 1961 that put Nevada in it's present #1 position.

Nevada has an incredible amount of federal land (over 85%) that is managed by the BLM and US Forest Service. This vast amount of open land provides excellent opportunities for gold prospectors. There are many areas that have surface gold deposits that can be located with a detector, and I have no doubt that there are still many isolated gold deposits that have not yet been discovered. Every county in the state of Nevada has gold, but much of the gold is so fine that extraction is not feasible for small-scale prospectors. Better to stick to areas that produce larger sized gold that have produced nuggets. As always, research is key to identifying these areas.

Some of the richest mines in Nevada only produce microscopic gold, while there are many long-forgotten mining towns that still have gold nuggets hiding nearby. For nugget hunting, Northern Nevada is definitely a favorite area to explore.

One of the very best areas to mine in Nevada is in Pershing County. Dry washers were used by the early miners, but today metal detectors are successful in locating nuggets. Rye Patch Placers has produced quite a bit of gold since it was discovered in 1938. Seven Troughs, Rabbit Hole, Sawtooth and Placerites are popular with metal detectorists as the gold is only a few feet from the surface on the bedrock.

A couple of other good areas are Willow Creek and Dun Glen. A lot of the gold here is from lode mines, and coarse specimen gold has been found in the area. It would also be worth your time to try the Rochester, Sierra, Unionville and Humboldt Districts. This county is so gold-rich that there is almost guaranteed to be a lot of gold left in the ground.

Humboldt County in the northern part of the state produces very large nuggets. Old drywash piles can be metal detected productively, as drywashing lost a lot of gold nuggets. Some noteworthy areas: Dutch Flats, Varyville, Rebel Creek, Winnemucca, Gold Run, Awakening, Paradise Valley and Warm Springs Districts.

Elko County, in the northeastern part of the state, has many mining districts producing both gold and silver. The northern part of the county, which is close to the Idaho border, contains the richest prospecting areas. Check out the Alder District by Wildhorse Reservoir; Sheridan and Columbia Creeks in the Aura District; Badger Creek, 76 Creek and the Bruneau River in the Charleston District of the Jarbidge Range; Coleman and Hammond Canyons; Van Duzer District near Mountain City; and many other districts scattered all through the county. Lode mining produces the most gold in the county.

Considerable mining has taken place in central and southern Nevada as well, although these areas are generally considered less productive for metal detecting than the gold districts in the northern parts of the state. Nevertheless, many areas might still be worth exploring.

In Washoe County thousands of ounces of gold came out of the Olinghouse District. Some of this gold is extracted in intricate crystalline formations that are highly valued by collectors.

There are plenty of opportunities in White Pine County, and exploration there has been limited due to the remote areas and harsh climate. Bald Mountain District is located in the northwest part of the county and some good sized nuggets have been found there. The Osceola District has been heavily mined hydraulically in Dry Gulch, and there is lode and placer gold near Ely, Nevada.

Nevada is over 85% public land, most of which is open to prospecting.

Esmeralda County has the Goldfield District south of Tonopah, which has produced lode deposits worth several million ounces of gold. Although a lot of the gold came from lodes. the Chinese worked some placers in the 1870s in the Klondyke, Sylvania, Silver Peak, Divide, Tule Canyon and Tokop areas. I have seen high-grade gold specimens that were found in Goldfield that were found by metal detecting that are worth thousands of dollars.

Mining in the Searchlight Mining District began in 1897 following the establishment of the Duplex mines. At its peak, the town had about 44 gold mines. Most of the mines closed down in the 1920s due to lack of rich ore.

Idaho

Idaho is an awesome place to prospect. Over 2/3 of Idaho is public BLM and Forest Service land, which is open to prospecting for the most part. You can find gold all over Idaho, with most of the gold mining regions covering the western part of the the state.

The mother of all Idaho discoveries was in 1862, with the Boise Basin gold strike. Recovery from that region counted in the millions of ounces of gold, and included several small mining towns that still exist today, including Placerville, Pioneerville, Centerville, and the largest being Idaho City.

Although the area is not noted for producing big nuggets, all the streams produced placer gold by bucket line dredging or hydraulic mining. Some large examples of gold in quartz have been discovered weighing over a pound, and a lot of these specimens ended up being rejected by the dredges and now sit in the tailing piles.

Atlanta, at the foot of the Sawtooth Mountains, also produced good amounts of placer and lode gold. Located in Elmore County, there is a lot left to find. All waters produce and are worth your time. Areas of note in Elmore County are Pine and Featherville.

The Boise Basin was Idaho's largest gold strike producing over 3 million ounces of gold, mostly from placer deposits. There are miles and miles of dredge tailings throughout the area that detectorists have found nuggets and nice gold/quartz specimens over the years.

The Yankee Fork still contains a significant amount of placer gold. Gold was discovered here in 1870 and the towns of Bonanza and Custer were built up to accommodate the miners. Still, mining was on and off for several decades as new mining technologies were discovered. In the mid-1900s, the Yankee Fork Gold Dredge churned up the valley and recovered millions of dollars in gold. Today, some gold prospectors still frequent the area, and it is a popular place for tourist visiting the nearby Sawtooth Mountains, Stanley, and Redfish Lake. The gold is mostly fine, but small nuggets and specimens can be recovered.

The Yankee Fork Dredge is open for tours during the summer months. When I was there in 2018, the Forest Service was reclaiming many of the old tailing piles to enhance riparian habitat along the river.

In remote Owyhee County, Silver was discovered on War Eagle Mountain in the Owyhee Mountains, bringing thousands of miners into the area from 1864 forward. There a few seasonal creeks, and Jordan Creek is the main gold-bearing tributary. Silver City is worth the trip just to see a fine example of an Idaho ghost town. Although it is home to quite a few year-round residents, there are examples of some fine old buildings, and you can see some interesting old mining equipment.

The Florence mining district is located in the central portion of the state. The mining season is short due to the high elevation, meaning that the snows come early and melt late. Also the area is pretty rugged terrain.

Elk City was the heart to the mining activities on Elk Creek, Red River and the South Fork of the Clearwater River. First mining was done by hand, then later by bucket line dredges. The area has gained some interest from recreational miners who can still find lots of gold left behind. There is lots of gold in this area, and it is remote. If you are feeling adventurous you can venture south and explore several small mining districts like the Dixie, Orogrande and Buffalo Hump. Go prepared, this is remote country!

Murray was the site of the last true "gold rush" in the lower-48. Gold in Pritchard Creek was discovered in the 1880s causing one of Idaho's major gold rushes. Actually, considering the richness of the area it is quite surprising that this area was not discovered sooner. Today place gold can be found in many places around Murray including Pritchard Creek, Eagle Creek, Beaver Creek, and Trail Creek among others. I've seen some big multi-ounce gold nuggets that were mined from the Murray area.

Pierce was home the first gold rush in Idaho. Gold was mined in Orofino Creek and the surrounding areas for a few years before all the buzz died down. However, this discovery brought in many miners who eventually discovered gold in other places throughout the state. Today the mountains surrounding Orofino Creek still contain lots of gold and many prospectors have reported success in these areas.

Successful nugget hunters in Idaho will have the best luck searching the old tailings, scanning in direct proximity of the old workings, and checking exposed ground adjacent to creeks and rivers. I have metal detected in Idaho quite a bit over the years, and I've found that the mining towns located in the timbered areas have a lot of soil and pine duff that covers up the gold and keep it out of reach of your detector. Finding sites with exposed ground is very important.

Montana

The western part of Montana is a rugged mountainous area along the Continental Divide, and is much richer than the remaining part of the state which is primarily flat prairie land.

Although gold was discovered in 1852, it wasn't until 1862 when the Grasshopper Creek strike brought in the prospectors by the thousands. West of Dillon the town of Bannack sprang up and the entire area was placer mined. In Alder Gulch at Virginia City, very large gold deposits were located the following year. The Rivers and Creeks near Virginia City and Bannack are still a good bet, but finding open ground will be a challenge.

Near Butte, Montana at the headwaters of the Clark Fork of the Columbia River there has been significant copper mining, and gold production is a byproduct. Weighing over 25 ounces, the Highland Centennial Nugget was found close to Butte. I own an interesting electrum specimen (an alloy of approximately 60% gold and 40% silver) that weighs about 1/2 an ounce that was found near Butte.

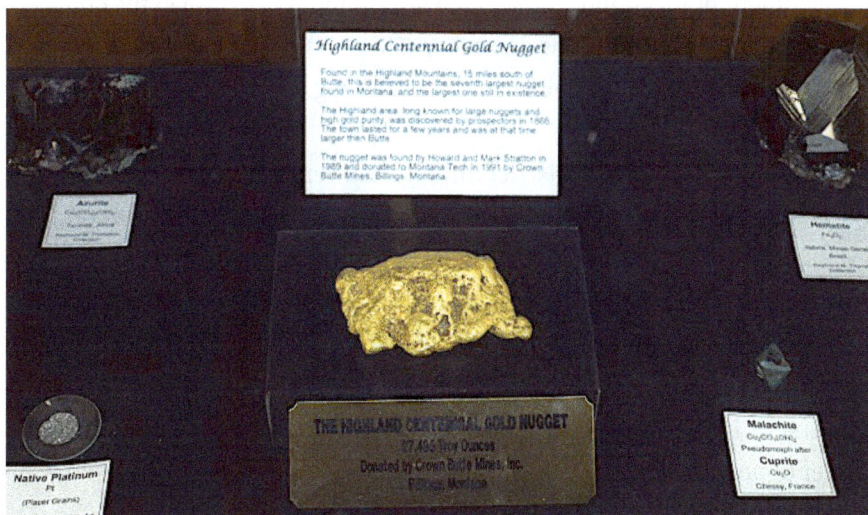

The Highland Centennial Nugget was found in the Highland Mountains south of Butte, Montana in 1989. It is on display at the Mineral Museum at Montana Tech.

The site of the Last Chance Gulch gold strike, along the Missouri River near Helena. The town is literally built on top of some of the richest mining ground in the entire state. As was often done, miners would set up camp close to the goldfields. As time went by the town expanded and covered more ground. The old downtown section of Helena is right on top of some rich gold-bearing gravel. Look around the hills and gulches just south of town and you will see all sorts of historic miner diggings.

One of the richest placers ever in the history of the state is **Confederate Gulch** between Helena and Townsend, east of the Missouri River. Some miners were finding over $1000 in one pan. Boulder Creek, Montana Gulch, Cement Gulch and Montana Bar had lucrative hydraulic operations.

Gold was first discovered in Libby Creek back in 1867, back when Montana was remote and unwelcoming. The climate, particularly during the winter months, can be harsh and unforgiving. This undoubtedly had an effect on the development of this remote area, but a few hundred men mined the creek for the first decade following the discovery. There is now an large section of the creek that is set aside for public gold prospecting.

Silver Creek in the Ottawa District initially had very rich placer deposits, and there have also been many lodes located there that were found later on.

North of Yellowstone National Park is the Jardine District, with hard rock deposits and also some placer gold.

The creeks in the Radersburg of the Elkhorn Mountains provide some good placer opportunities.

There is some gold in the central part of the state in the Kendall and North Moccasin Districts, but most of the gold found is primarily low grade ores.

There are many more small mining towns throughout Montana that have good potential for nugget hunting. To my knowledge, the 25-ounce Highland Centennial Nugget is the largest existing nugget from Montana, but I know that many nuggets that were even larger were found by the early miners. Many weighing over a pound have been documented.

New Mexico

Although New Mexico doesn't come close to the gold production of neighboring Arizona, it has produced a decent amount of both placer and lode gold. Production was difficult in the early days of discovery, as the Apache Indians were a deterrent to the Mexican Settlers and Spanish explorers who found gold there.

Most of the gold produced today is a byproduct of other mining operations, but there is still some left for the amateur prospector to find. It's rare to find a large gold nugget in New Mexico. Even in the known gold mining areas, most of the gold nuggets will be <1 gram. Keep that in mind when you choose a metal detector. A detector with good sensitivity on small gold will be very important if you want to be successful here.

Gold prospecting in New Mexico can be difficult because it is an extremely dry state. Pans, sluices and dredges won't work where there is no water, but this is not problem for detectorists. In fact, areas that were only marginally worked or failed to be profitable for the early miners can be successfully hunted with metal detectors.

In southwestern New Mexico, the Hillsboro District produced quite a bit of gold in dry placers in the gulches. The history of Hillsboro dates back nearly 150 years now with a town that was founded in 1877 after gold was discovered on the Mimbres Mountains along Percha Creek. More locations were found that contained rich silver, gold, and copper deposits. Most of the richest ground was found to the northwest of town, toward Copper Peak and Empire Peak.

Placer gold deposits were mined in Percha Creek, Ready Pay Gulch, Wicks Gulch, Warm Springs Canyon, and Grayback Arroyo. Good gold could be recovered from many of the feeder gulches that drained them, and many lodes were discovered by miners who traced them back to their source.

A few miles north of Silver City, the Pinos Altos is a dry placer area, and Whiskey, Rich and Santo Domingo gulches all have gold, as well as Bear Creek which has placer gold.

Southwest of Santa Fe is Old Placers, where the Delores and Cunningham gulches have both produced for miners using drywashers. Nearby is an area called New Placers that produced extremely pure gold.

Elizabethtown was the epicenter of one of New Mexico's most productive gold mining district during the early days of gold mining in the state. The most productive areas included Humbug Creek, Grouse Creek, all along the western slopes of Mount Baldy and Moreno River among others. Many large nuggets have been found on the eastern side of the Mount Baldy. Willow Creek was especially productive. Many places around the town are also known to contain rich gravels where you can dig for gold.

On the eastern side of Mount Baldy are the Baldy placers. You can find good areas to search at Ute, Willow and South Ponil Creeks.

Much of New Mexico is private land, Indian Reservations and military reserves and these will require permission to prospect, or may be off limits altogether. Make sure you know the rules, and respect the claims on public lands as well. Getting permission from owners and claim holders ahead of time will make things easier for you.

Colorado

Colorado is an interesting state for gold hunters. There is an incredibly rich gold mining history here, and the opportunities for gold prospectors is quite impressive. However, most of the gold in Colorado is very fine textured and not suitable to be found with a metal detector. Most of the gold-bearing creeks and rivers contain fine gold dust more suitable for panning and sluicing.

For detectorists, the best chance of finding gold is by hunting the ore piles from the countless lode mines scattered across the states. Rather than focusing on trying to find nuggets, you will likely have the best odds of success hunting for rich veins and specimens that were missed by the old-timers.

The Pike's Peak Gold Rush took off after big discoveries near Denver in 1858. Gold mining has been one of Colorado's most significant industries ever since, lode and placer.

Park County has produced over a million ounces of gold, primarily through lode mining. However at the headwaters of the South Platte River, along with nearby tributaries, the Fairplay District was a pretty rich placer mining area.The east range of the Mosquito Mountains and the Tarryall District have all produced gold. There is a gold display at the Denver Museum of Nature ans Science that houses several large placer gold nuggets, including the largest known to have been found in Colorado weighing 12 troy ounces! Another piece on display weighs almost 8 troy ounces. Both of these were found in the Alma Mining District in Park County.

Gilpin County west of Denver has produced a major amount of the gold coming out of Colorado. Four million ounces of gold has come out of the Central City District alone, primarily from lode deposits.

The Cripple Creek District produces the most gold in Colorado and is one of the highest producing areas in the country. There are quite a few large mines still in operation here producing lode gold, including Cripple Creek and Victor Gold Mines. Although there are fewer placer deposits here, once again, it would be worth a look.

Summit County in central Colorado has produced over 1 million ounces of gold – both lode and placer deposits. One of the richest parts of Colorado is the Breckenridge District. with a significant amount of the gold production coming from gravel beds that are mined hydraulically. Breckenridge is an area known for producing a unique type of wiry, leafy, crystalline gold. These pieces are usually very small, but bigger pieces do exist. Some of the best specimens clearly weigh several pounds that are on display at the Denver Museum of Nature and Science. A massive chunk of gold, nicknamed "Tom's Baby" was found at the Gold Flake Mine and weighs 156 ounces!

Colorado isn't widely known for producing large gold, but there are exceptions! "Tom's Baby" is a 156-ounce crystalline gold nugget that was found near Breckenridge. Many large crystalline gold specimens have been found in this area, and are on display that the Denver Museum of Nature and Science.

Many placer locations in Lake County along the Arkansas River and some of its tributaries can still be productive. Keep an eye out for old placer workings. The gulches and streams of the Leadville District has numerous mines.

Much of this states gold is locked up in rocks and found as very fine veins of gold within quartz and other matrix. Scanning those ore piles is a good way to find high-grade specimen material at old mining sites. Detecting steep scree slopes with scattered ore is not for the faint of heart, but hard work can turn of some incredible specimens that are highly valued by collectors.

Wyoming

Wyoming is the most sparsely populated and remote state in the nation, so it stands to reason that it has not been as well explored than other areas. There has been gold found in Wyoming since 1842 by pioneers heading west.

The Sierra Madre and Medicine Bow Mountains located in the south-central section of Wyoming were prospected until the end of the great depression. There are quite a few mines in the region, and many were not worked out, they were just abandoned due to low gold prices. Given the price of gold today, these areas could definitely be worth further investigation.

There are low grade gold ores in the Granite Mountain Range, Rattlesnake Hills, Tin Cup, and Seminoe District, located in the center of the state. Although not commercially viable, you might have some luck here.

The Silver Crown, Esterbrook, Warbonnet and Garrett in the Laramie Mountain Range have some districts worth taking a look at.

To the south end of the Wind River Range is the South Pass-Atlantic City District, with some other districts including Oregon Buttes, Twin Creek and Lewiston. South Pass City saw its population boom, and it owes it all to gold.

In 1867, a miner rode into Great Salt Lake City with an interesting find, **a** crushed quartz rock that held 40 ounces of gold dust. The gold ore was refined into a bar worth $740, with a fineness of 934.5. The discovery was published in the Utah newspaper, and locals rushed 200 miles northeast in what would be the beginning of Wyoming's gold rush.

Several new mines began springing up as the city was established, but the Carissa Mine was the principal mine and the richest in terms of deposits. Half a mile away from South Pass City, it was originally called the Carissa ledge. It was this rich shelf that produced the original discovery. For metal detecting, this area probably holds the best potential for nugget hunters.

Other mines in the area, though not as rich as the Carissa Mine, also produced a good amount of precious metal. Within a few miles of South Pass City are the Franklin Mine, Shields Mine, B & H Mine, Barr Mine, and King Soloman Mine.

Just over the hill at Atlantic City were several other active mining operations. They included the Duncan Mine, St. Louis Mine, Mary Ellen Mine, Diana Mine, and Garfield Mine. Countless smaller prospects can be found in the hills above Rock Creek.

Fortunately, the state of Wyoming has vast amounts of public land, and most of which is open for exploring.

South Dakota

In 1874 gold was discovered by a group of men under General Custer at French Creek in South Dakota which later became Custer County. Not being too concerned that the Black Hills area was still owned by the Sioux, prospectors were soon busy trying to get rich.

Whitewood and Deadwood Creeks proved to be rich in placer gold. The town of Deadwood soon grew up around the rich gold area, which was an illegal settlement known as one of the most dangerous places to live and work in the country. As Deadwood had no particular law and order in evidence, prospectors took their chances.

As the miners expanded their search they found some extremely rich placer creeks and also some lode sources that proved very profitable. There are plenty of streams in Custer County that will produce gold.

Near the Wyoming border to the west, the Black Hills will probably be the profitable area to search. Millions of ounces have come from Custer, Lawrence and Pennington counties, and even though they've been mined, you can still find quite a bit.

Lawrence County is the home of the Homestake Mine, producing over 20 million ounces of gold over its lifetime. Strawberry, Elk and Deadwood creeks all have placer gold, as well as Yellow, Squaw and Annie creeks. There are quite a few lode mines near the town of Lead, and many of the creeks and gulches have been worked.

South Dakota legend John Perrett with a 7.43 troy ounce gold nugget that he found at Potato Creek in 1929.

Pennington County has seen less gold produced than Lawrence County, but that doesn't mean it should be ignored. Located in the Black Hills to the south, there are some abandoned and some active mines in the area, and Castle, Battle, Spring and Rapid creeks will all show placer gold.

While there are is certainly plenty of gold left to find, be aware that the area around the Black Hills is still heavily claimed. Despite being some of the richest gold deposits in the world, the mineralized region in South Dakota where mining has occurred is relatively small, only covering a fairly small percentage of the state. Towns like Deadwood and Lead now rely on tourism more than mining.

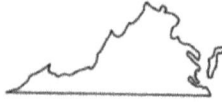

Virginia

There are a handful of states in the East with a rich mining history, and Virginia is definitely one of them. Most of that gold comes from the "gold-pyrite" belt approximately 9 to 15 miles wide, running 140 miles along the Blue Ridge Mountains' eastern side. Other mines outside of the belt exist also. Gold can still be located in any of the places where gold was found in the past.

Thomas Jefferson found gold in Virginia way back in 1782, well before any of the major gold rushes would occur. Over the coming century, miners would find many rich gold deposits throughout the state.

The gold that Thomas Jefferson referenced finding in 1782 was a 17-pennyweight piece of gold ore that was picked up along the Rappahannock River. This ore was likely found in the area where the White Hall Mine in Spotsylvania County would eventually begin operations. Although limited information exists about the early workings of the mine, it is known that considerable gold was found here.

Beginning in 1828, the state averaged about 3000 ounces per year, with a record year over 6000 ounces. At its peak, there were several hundred mines being worked in Virginia. A good number of these were hard rock mines, extracting free-milling gold that was extracted, crushed and processed to recover the gold.

Gold mining continued in Virginia up until the start of the Civil War. After the war, mining continued on a much smaller scale for many decades.

Within the belt long the Blue Ridge Mountains are good bets for the prospector, as placer gold can be found in many of the rivers and creeks. Stick with the historically mined areas. The counties noted for their mining history include: Prince Edward, Fluvanna, Cumberland, Buckingham, Facquier, Madison, Culpepper, Orange and Louisa Counties.

Facquier County is home of the Franklin Mine, which is one of the most famous in Virginia. It began operating in 1825, and for the first year gold was plentiful near the surface of the ground. Strip mining was productive and produced over $1,000,000 in gold in just the first few years. Fires and flooding slowed things down, but operations continued on-and-off for many decades and even up through the Great Depression.

There are many other lode mines in the southeastern section of Facquier County.

Heading to the west, Caroll County and Dinwiddie County in the southeast has hard rock deposits scattered throughout the area.

A rich placer gold deposit was found near Little Byrd Creek in Goochland County. Hydraulic mining was done early on to strip away overburden and expose bedrock for miners. In later years a dragline dredge was brought in to process gravels.

Today there is very little active mining taking place in Virginia. Many of the best sources of gold have been depleted too much to attract attention from commercial interests, but modern-day prospectors can still find some gold in many of these places. Placer mining is more common than metal detecting, but there are nuggets and specimens here that can be found with a detector. Many of the nuggets are very high purity and quite beautiful.

North Carolina

North Carolina has the distinction of having the very first documented discovery of gold in the United States at the Reed Gold Mine. Since the discovery in 1799 gold has been located primarily as lode deposits and byproducts from mining for other minerals.

Running in a diagonal line across the state is the Carolina Slate Belt, where most of the North Carolina gold is found. This line starts in the northwest around Caswell, Person and Granville counties and ends up in the southwest around Gaston, Meckenburg and Union counties.

In Granville County there are placers in the streams, but most gold production is as a byproduct from the copper mines. There are good placer streams in Person and Caswell counties as well.

Toward the south, the Hoover Hill Mine is located in Randolph County. It produced great amounts of gold and there are rich placer deposits in the Uwharrie River nearby.

Historically, a lot of gold was produced in Stanly, Union and Cabarrus Counties. Check out the Rocky River for placer gold, as well as all the waters in the area. There are a lot of lode gold mines in the area, and around the Reed Gold Mine some pretty big nuggets have been found.

With a high quality metal detector you might have some pretty good luck in this area. I have seen some very nice specimen gold recovered from hard rock mines in North Carolina. Placer gold can be recovered from many creeks and rivers throughout the state.

Similarly, there are lode deposits here and there, and all the waters will potentially produce gold in Davidson County, as well as Montgomery County close by. The Uwharrie River and tributaries has produced placer gold and is worth checking out.

There is definitely a lot of gold left in North Carolina. With the history of large gold nuggets being found (including nuggets and ore specimens weighing many pounds at the Reed Mine), metal detecting certainly has potential.

You should know that most of the areas in the state that have gold are on private property. Get permission before you start, and be respectful of the areas that you are working in.

South Carolina

You will be most successful if you target your efforts within the Carolina Slate Belt that runs approximately 125 miles inland and parallel to the Pacific Ocean.

This belt begins in Lancaster County in the north, although it actually starts in the southern part of Virginia. Heading southwest to Edgefield County, the belt continues through parts of Georgia and includes both South and North Carolina.

The Haile Mine, which is one of the biggest mines in the southeastern US, is located in Lancaster County. This one lode mine alone has yielded over ¼ million ounces, and there are many other mines scattered through Lancaster County. All the waters near the mines will probably have placer gold.

Moving west to York County there are many lode mines, and the waters should all be profitable. In particular, take a look at the Broad River and tributaries, and in Fairfield County, check out the Little River.

Some other possible areas are Cherokee County and Chesterfield County, focusing on Nugget Creek. How can you go wrong with a name like that! Also take a look at the Little Saluda River and tributaries in Saluda County.

The Dorn Mine was one of the noted and most productive of the South Carolina gold mines in the 19th century. William Dorn, an Edgefield County farmer, discovered what would become one of the richest veins of gold in South

Carolina's history in 1852. Dorn Mine was a pocket mine that was closed after extracting close to $3,000,000 worth of gold.

There were rich lode and placer mines in Greenville County. The most noteworthy were the Briggs and Wildcat Mines that produced lode gold; and the McBee Placer and Westmoreland Placer Mines which had rich placer gold.

Southeast from the town of Verdery in Greenwood County, placer gold was found along many of the streams in the area, including Little Muckaway Creek and Beaverdam Creek. Nearby to the town of Troy, lode gold was produced by the Young Mine.

Placer gold yield from these two mines was double that of the lode mines in the surrounding area. Martin Mine near Smyrna is also pretty notable and its biggest claim to fame was the sizable gold nuggets found in the mine. In 1856, two large gold nuggets weighing 9.5 ounces and 17 ounces were found at the Martin mine.

The Henderson Prospect and other gold mines in the towns of Honea Path and Williamston in Anderson County have produced placer gold. Mines in Honea Path relied upon minor gold finds in Chinquola Mill Creek, and placers were also worked around Williamston on Camp Creek and many surrounding drainage.

Georgia

Georgia is definitely the most famous gold mining state in the Southeast. So much gold was found here that the US Government even established the Dahlonega Mint, which produced gold coins between 1838 to 1861.

The largest concentration of gold was found in northern Cherokee, Lumpkin and White counties. Surprisingly, assays of gold in Georgia often turn out to be well above 23 karats, some of the purest natural gold deposits found anywhere on Earth. As with other southeastern states, gold here can be found in both lode and placer deposits.

Rich placer gold deposits were found in the Etowah and Little Rivers in Cherokee County. The county has also produced large quantities of lode gold that was mine by the Cherokee and Sixes Mines. This area will still produce plenty of gold today.

Southeast of Ball Ground on the Etowah River were numerous area prospects and mines, like the Franklin-Creighton Mine, in exposures of decomposed bedrock.

The Sixes Mine are a large group of mines located near Sixes. Several mines are located in this area including the 301 Mine, Cherokee Mine, Clarkston Mine, Downing Creek Mine, Macou, and Putnam Mines. This is a significant gold producing area that has been worked since the start of the gold rush to Georgia.

All the stream and bench gravels contain placer gold around the town of Cumming, especially in James Creek, which flows into the Chattahoochee River. Two miles east of the city was the site where an old hydraulic mining operation was worked.

Northwest of Forsyth County, near the boundary with Gwinnett County in Sugar Hill, was the location of the Simmons Mines, a productive lode gold mine in the area.

The county's largest waterway is the Tallapoosa River, which flows from its northeastern to southwestern corner. This is very rich country, where placer gold deposits occur throughout the tributaries within the county.

The numerous rich placer gold locations for this historic mining region were situated in all of the regional creeks draining into the Chattahoochee River near Gainesville.

Lumpkin County, which originated and formed as a part of Hall County, was the site where gold was first discovered in Georgia. The historic ghost town of Auraria, and the celebrated county seat of Dahlonega in Lumpkin County were the principal sites that attracted attention. For a time, this part of Georgia was getting more focus from gold miners than anywhere in the entire world.

The Chestatee River had numerous mines along its banks, with rich placer gold deposits found throughout. Likewise, the Etowah River contained placer gold, together with its smaller creeks and tributaries like the Baggs, McClusky and Calhoun Creeks.

The nearby Tesnatee River was also a respectable producer of gold, and so was the Yahoola Creek, located in the city of Dahlonega, now the county seat of Lumpkin County. There are other unnamed tributaries in Dahlonega that carried significant quantities of gold as well.

Alabama

Many folks have no idea just how much gold has been found in Alabama. Gold discovered in Alabama has been mined from both placer and lode sources.

The goldfields were primarily found in a gold belt covering an area of 60 miles wide and 100 miles long, situated on the Eastern border with Georgia near the cities of Birmingham and Montgomery. This area is basically the southern extent of the Carolina Slate Belt that extends across the southern states.

The foremost strike of gold occurred in 1830 along the tributaries of Blue and Chestnut Creeks in Chilton County. This discovery made Alabama one of the prolific gold-producing states east of the Mississippi River, with almost 80,000 ounces of gold since 1830.

Most of the gold in the heart of the state has been produced at the Hog Mountain District and the eastern banks of the Hillabee Creek in Talapoosa County. Both locations, together with Cleburne County were credited to produce the bulk of Alabama's gold.

In Cleburne County, the Anna Howe Mines are thought to have produced the first gold-bearing quartz in Alabama. It made the county one of the most prolific producers of gold in the state. Other gold bearing streams can be found around Arbacoochee and Chulafinnee. Parts of Hillabee Creek will also produce gold within Cleburne County.

Chilton county sourced its gold from several streams and tributaries that flowed towards Coosa River in Clanton City and the small town of Verbena.

The southwestern portion of the Alabama gold belt included parts of Chilton County. Gold nuggets were reported to have been recovered in Clanton, particularly from Blue Creek, a short tributary of the Coosa River in the southeastern part of Chilton County.

In Clay County, placer gold occurred at the Wesobulga Creek, Crooked Creek, Tallapoosa River, and several unnamed streams throughout the county.

Along the far west side of Randolph County and the far east side of Clay County lies the Cragford district. Several mines operating here produced free-milling gold from veins in quartz. Properties situated along the tributaries of Crooked Creek have both placer and lode gold deposits.

In the western part of the county is the Idaho district. The Eley, Haraldson, Shinker, Alabama Gold and Mica Company, Prospect Tunnel and Harall Gold Mines all operated in this area, which contained lode gold. Placers can be found in Hillabee Creek and many of the smaller drainages in this area.

Coosa County has extensive placer gold prospect areas with a significant history of mining during the early gold rush days in Alabama. Rich placer gold occurred along Weogufka Creek and Hatchet Creek.

In Talladega County, the Riddle Mine and the Woodward Tract in the south-eastern part of the county, and the Story Mine south of the county on the eastern flank of the Talladega Creek, have all produced lode gold in quartz veins from decomposed rocks and slates, with placer gold found in area branches and benches along the Talladega Creek.

Tallapoosa County composed four principal gold districts: Goldville, Hog Mountain, Eagle Creek and Devil's Backbone. Miners worked out for placer gold deposits in the shoal sands and stream gravels in watercourses, like in the streams of Owl Hollow Valley, Long Branch Creek, Channahatchee Creek, Kowaliga Creek, Copper Creek and the headwaters of the Peru Creek. Several of these streams are now part and lie under the waters of Lake Martin, a reservoir formed through the construction of the Martin Dam on the Tallapoosa River.

The Talladega National Forest contained several creeks, where placer gold also occurs. Of course many of the richest mining areas are located on private ground, but the National Forest lands do provide potential metal detecting opportunities for the public.

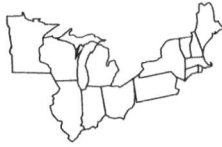

Miscellaneous Other States

There are a handful of other states that have a small possibility of producing nugget-sized gold if you search the right areas. Nearly every state in the US has gold, but most other states not listed above will only produce small gold dust. Finding detectable gold will be a challenge.

For example, most of the states in the northern 1/3 of the country have glacial gold deposits. This is gold that has been transported down from Canada through glacial movement. Any area with glacial gold could *hypothetically* have a nugget, but the reality is that these deposits are almost always super, *super* fine textured. Never say never, but finding a nugget with your detector in these areas would be equivalent to the needle in the haystack.

Maine has a few areas that have produced gold nuggets. Gold can be found throughout the Swift River and many of its tributaries. Although most of the gold found here is very fine, the Swift River is one of the locations in Maine where you have a possibility of finding some nice flakes and maybe even a gold nugget or two. There is a popular gold panning area on the East Branch Swift River a short distance from the town of Byron.

Gold is found in both **New Hampshire** and **Vermont**. Again, most of the gold is fine textured, but occasional "picker" sized nuggets are found. In New Hampshire check out Tunnel Brook in Benton, Wild Ammunoosuc River in Lisbon, Salmon Hole Brook in Lisbon, Notch Brook in Lincoln and Baker River draining into the Merrimack River.

Michigan mostly has fine glacial gold deposits not suitable for hunting with a metal detector. However, one notable exception is the Ropes Mine in Michigan's Upper Peninsula. The mine was founded by the man named Julius Ropes who discovered gold among the serpentine rocks located in the northern region of Ishpeming in 1881. This mine was never exceptionally rich, and it operated on-and-off for over a century since the initial discovery. A modest amount of gold was recovered, but the deposits were low-grade ore and probably not suitable for detecting.

Maryland has a surprisingly rich gold mining history. Gold was first discovered in the state in early 1800s. Although gold was discovered much earlier in Maryland, no commercial mining was commenced until after the Civil War. In fact, after the Civil War, the state was heavily prospected for gold with a few commercially viable being found in the Piedmont Plateau.

The majority of the gold that has been recovered here is found in the northern and central parts of the state. Peak recorded production of over 1000 ounces of gold just prior to World War II. While most mines in Maryland are now abandoned, at one time they were actively recovering gold from hard rock sources. Urban development most likely limits the potential for future prospecting efforts in Maryland.

There is a small but rich area in southeastern **Tennessee** that is worth mentioning. The best area to pan is the southeastern corner near the towns of Tellico Plains and Coker Creek. Extending through the area near the borders of North Carolina and Tennessee is the gold belt, and Coker Creek (not the town, but the actual creek) is the most well-known place to have a look.

A short gold rush began there in 1831, and the prospectors found gravels that were not productive enough to make it worth their while. Although there wasn't enough gold to interest commercial mining ventures, this area has seen a lot of interest from small-scale prospectors in recent years.

Utah has fairly lackluster opportunities for the nugget hunter. With a vast amount of public land and its proximity to rich states like Arizona and Nevada, one would expect it would be a prospectors paradise. Truth be told, I don't think I've ever heard of or seen a gold nugget of any size that has been found in Utah.

The Bingham Copper Mine produces massive quantities of gold, but all as a by-product from their copper mining operations. Historic mining has taken place on the Colorado River, Green River and San Juan River, but these deposits are all very fine. A few deposits occur in the Abajo Mountain at Recapture and Johnson Creeks that may be worthy of further research. I'm sure there are a few nuggets somewhere in Utah, but it will take some serious effort to find them.

Researching Potential Prospecting Areas

The Importance of Research

In the last chapter, we just scratched the surface on some of the best areas in the US to metal detect for gold nuggets. This information was intended to simply get you started in your research, but there is a lot more to learn before you head out into the field.

Truth be told, every successful nugget hunter I've ever known has been obsessed with research. They area constantly studying old books, reports and mining literature for little snippets of information that may lead them to the next area to prospect.

Once they get a rough idea for an area they want to explore, they dig deeper, finding every bit of information they can find on their specific area. They pour over maps to get a feel for the general landscape, research accessibility and get a well-rounded view of the area before they head out into the field. To be a successful nugget hunter, the research is almost as important as the detector itself.

Books

With a small amount of research, you should be able to locate a general area that has produced gold. There are many books with good information on various states, and there is an abundance of information available on the internet nowadays. Doing a search on Amazon.com for your state, for example: "Gold in (State)" will likely pull up at least one, and probably several books on the subject. These books often contain detailed maps, mineralogy studies, and accounts of past gold discoveries.

Armed with this information, aspiring prospectors can strategically narrow down their search to the most promising locations, saving precious time and resources. Here are just a few examples of books and printed reports that I was able to find for the state of Arizona with very little effort:

- Gold in Arizona: A Prospector's Guide by Dan Hausel
- Lode Gold Mining in Arizona by Arizona Bureau of Mines
- Placer Gold Mining in Arizona by US Geological Survey
- Directory of Operating Mines in Arizona in 1915 by Arizona Bureau of Mines
- Gold Placers and Placering in Arizona: Bulletin #168 by Eldred D Wilson
- Ghost Towns and Historical Haunts of Arizona by Thelma Heatwole
- Ghost Towns of Arizona by James E. Sherman

This is just a small sample of what is readily available for just one state.

Books about exploring old ghost towns is another great way to learn about the early mining history in your area. Ghost towns, particularly in the West, were often first established as mining camps that would grow to support the nearby mines. Many of these towns are long gone, lost to wildfires and to the hands of time. There many be nothing more that a few scattered relics left to indicate that they even existed, but some of them were once home to thousands of miners.

I do realize the irony of a gold prospecting book telling you the importance of buying more books, but what I'm trying to emphasize here is that **you can never have too much information** about the areas that you want to detect for gold. I have an entire bookshelf of research material that I reference often. Finding new areas to explore is every bit as important as your detecting skills.

Government Reports

Some of the best information on gold occurrences is found in a variety of government reports. Many of these reports are now digitally available online, or can be purchased as reprints from a variety of sellers. Many different agencies produced various reports on mining throughout history, but they are most commonly put out by the U.S. Geological Survey, Bureau of Land Management, or the various state-level agencies that manage mining and mineral resources.

Principal Gold-Producing Districts of the United States

By A. H. KOSCHMANN *and* M. H. BERGENDAHL

GEOLOGICAL SURVEY PROFESSIONAL PAPER 610

A description of the geology, mining history, and production of the major gold-mining districts in 21 States

These reports will almost always go more in-depth than most books. In fact, most of the more recently published gold prospecting books are usually sourcing their information from these old reports, so it's a good idea to go right to the original source.

Sometimes these reports will cover an entire state, but more commonly they cover the mineral resources within a specific county or mining district. Sometimes they will even be written about specific mines. The more information you can narrow down the broad information (like my summary in the last chapter) to find more about specific detailed locations, the better your odds of success.

Old Newspaper Articles

Finding old newspaper articles from 100 years ago can be an exciting journey into the past, but it requires a bit of detective work and resourcefulness. Here's a step-by-step guide to help you in your quest:

1. **Identify the Newspapers:** Determine which newspapers were in circulation during the time of the early gold rushes in the area are highly relevant to the area you're interested in. Local newspapers are more likely to cover regional events and stories of that time, and during that time most of the economy in most areas was based around logging, mining and ranching. National or major newspapers may have archived articles available, but local papers often provide more detailed and specific information.

2. **Check Online Newspaper Archives:** Many newspapers have been digitized and are available through online newspaper archives. These archives may be offered by libraries, historical societies, or commercial databases. Popular newspaper databases like Newspapers.com an Chronicling America can be valuable resources for accessing old articles.

3. **Visit Libraries and Archives:** Local libraries, historical societies, and

university archives often maintain physical collections of old newspapers. Visit these institutions and inquire about their holdings. Some may have microfilm or digitized versions available for public use. Librarians and archivists can be incredibly valuable guides in your research.

4. **Utilize Online Library Catalogs:** Some libraries and universities have digitized their collections or indexed old newspapers in their catalogs. Check their online databases or catalogs to see if any relevant material is available.

5. **Visit Newspaper Publishers:** If the newspaper you are interested in still exists, consider contacting the publisher's office. Some publishers maintain archives of their publications, and they might be willing to assist you in your search.

6. **Explore Historical Societies and Museums:** Local historical societies and museums might have collections of old newspapers or access to historical records. For smaller counties, contacting them directly to inquire about available resources is usually the most effective.

Remember that searching for old newspaper articles can require patience and persistence, but the insights and stories you uncover can provide a fascinating glimpse into the past and serve as a very valuable resource. This research method also takes more effort and patience, which means that it may lead you to tips that other prospectors have missed by only reading the well-known literature.

FRIDAY, DECEMBER 4, 1925

n Is Head Of
lic Buildings
ommittee

GENERAL FENG IS MOVING ON TIENTSIN

**American and British Gun-
boats Are Reported Now
at Chefoo**

By International News Service
LONDON, Dec. 4.—General Feng's army is moving on Tientsin with the intention of driving out the forces of General Li Ching Lin, who

42-Ounce Gold Nugget Discovery Excites Alaskans

By International News Service
ANCHORAGE, Alaska, Dec. 4. Excitement ran high here today after the discovery of a gold nugget weighing forty-three ounces by C. B. Nelson, a prospector. Nelson discovered the large nugget on the Kantishna river, about sixty miles west of Kobe. The nugget is valued at $731.

After borrowing enough money for a grubstake, Nelson returned to the scene of his find. His discovery is the third placer strike reported this season.

the support of the Soviet union. It

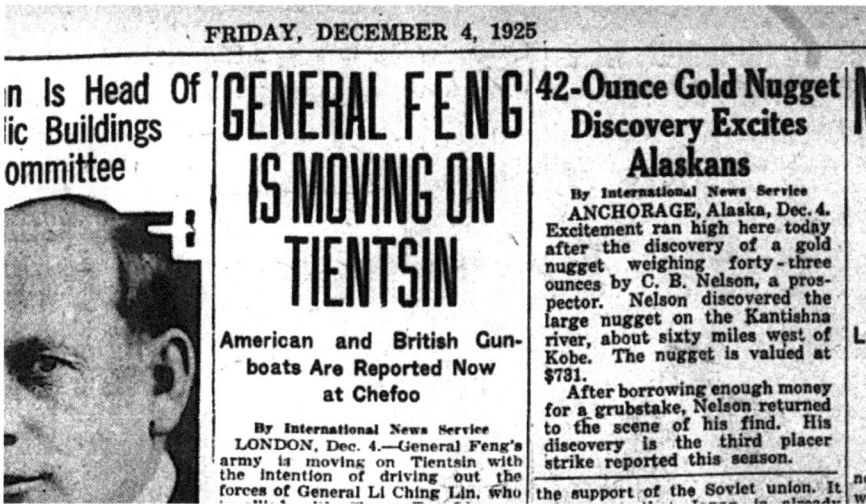

An old newspaper article from 1925 reporting about a gold nugget weighing several pounds that was mined from the Katishna River in Alaska. I found this by doing an online search on Chronicling America: Historic American Newspapers. This is a free online tool available through the Library of Congress. (chroniclingamerica.loc.gov)

Maps and Google Earth

Before doing any on-the-ground research, most successful gold prospectors today use some type of mapping program like Google Earth to locate potential prospecting areas. This is an excellent tool to help you find areas, even if you are hundreds of miles away in the comfort of your home.

Surface disturbances like dredge tailing and hydraulic washouts will show up clearly in these aerial photos, and you can use this in conjunction with maps and GPS to plot areas to investigate when you get there. You can also identify areas that would concentrate placer gold like bends in the river or large exposed boulders.

Just about every successful prospector I know uses Google Earth and other types of online mapping software to research study the aerial imagery of gold-bearing areas. This research is critical, because the aerial photos and topographical maps in combination with documented historical gold locations gives today's prospector an added advantage that the early gold miners never had.

What Information do you Focus on?

The detailed information provided within these books and government reports is invaluable for any gold prospector. But for those of us who are using a metal detector, one of the most important things to consider is the size that the gold occurs.

Metal detectors will only find gold of a certain size, and many rich gold areas do not have gold that is large enough to be detected. If the gold was fine textured gold dust, or low-grade gold ore, then other types of mining methods may be better suited for the area.

Gold detectorists are focused on two specific things; gold nuggets and high-grade gold specimens that are large enough to be found with a handheld metal detector. You can be standing on top of the richest gold mine in the world, but if the gold particles are not large enough then you're detector will be useless.

There are many rich mining areas that are like this. One of the biggest gold deposits on Earth are the Carlin Trend gold deposits in Northern Nevada. Billions of dollars worth of gold have been mined from this region, yet almost all of that gold is invisible to the human eye! That's right, even with a magnifying glass, you would not be able to see a solid speck of gold in the ore that is recovered from these huge mines because takes tons and tons of this low-grade ore to produce just one ounce of gold. These are *not* the areas that you want to seek out if you are metal detecting for gold nuggets.

Instead, you want to pay close attention to anything that mentions the *size of the gold* being found. Here is a examples of the type of information that I would be very interested in:

> *"Of the yield of these placers, anything like an approximation to the average daily amount of what was taken out per man would only be guess work. Hundreds of dollars per day to the man was common, and now and again a thousand or more a day. Don Juan Ferra took one nugget from his claim that weighed forty-seven ounces and six dollars. Another party found a chispa weighing twenty-seven ounces. Many others found pieces of from one to two ounces up to twenty, and yet it is contended that the greater proportion of the larger nuggets were never shown . . . . It is the opinion of those most con- versant with the first working of these placers that much the greater proportion of the gold taken out was in nuggets weighing from one dollar up to the size*

mentioned above .... As has been said above, the gold was large and generally clear of foreign substances .... All that was sold or taken here went for $16 to $17 an ounce."

Arizona Gold Placers and Placering - Arizona Bureau of Mines - discussing the La Paz Placers in West-central Yuma County, AZ.

Obviously, any mention of multi-ounce gold nuggets is going to get me very excited! Unfortunately, additional research indicates that this area is now part of the Colorado River Indian Reservation and would be off-limits to most prospectors.

Here's another interesting one:

"These placers occur in the stream channels and on certain of the intervening mesas of a roughly triangular area that extends for about 20 miles east and northeast from the head of Big Bug Creek. The gold of the stream placers is generally coarse. One of the largest nuggets found in the Big Bug region contained about $500 worth of gold..."

Arizona Gold Placers and Placering - Arizona Bureau of Mines discussing the Big Bug Placers in Yavapai County, AZ.

It's worthwhile to note a few things about this quote. First, the word "coarse" is commonly used in old mining literature. It can sometimes be used to describe the texture of the gold, but often it is more of a reference to the size of gold. Coarse gold is always something to pay attention to. Coarse gold is large enough to be found with your metal detector. Second, note that the values mentioned. Keep in mind that these reports were often written back when gold was worth considerably less. At the height of many of the gold rushes, the metal was valued at less than $20 per ounce. Even in the 1960s, gold was worth around $35 per ounce. A $500 nugget would have weighed over a pound!

Another interesting quote:

> *"In the upper part of Alder Gulch, much of the placer gold was "coarse, ragged, and little or not at all water worn" (Douglass, 1905, p. 354). Douglass also reported that a "decomposed vein" (the Lucas lode) below the upper placer ground yielded gold, and placer ground downstream from the vein was very rich, implying that the vein was surely the source of the placer gold. Douglass further stated that gold became progressively finer grained downstream to the mouth of the gulch, although some "fair-sized nuggets" were recovered near the mouth of the gulch. According to Browne (1868, p. 506), placer gold at the head of Alder Gulch is "coarse and rough, with portions of quartz adhering to it; further down the stream it becomes finer and brighter, showing unmistakable evidence of having been worn by the action of water. Near the mouth it is exceedingly fine [grained]." These relations are convincing evidence of a local source for much of the gold."*

Gold Deposits in the Virginia City-Alder Gulch District, Montana by Daniel R. Shaw and Kenneth L. Weir

The mention of "coarse, ragged" gold with "quartz adhering to it" is a great indication that it is of sufficient size for metal detecting. This information implies that the gold is likely sourced from a lode vein, with most of the larger gold being found closest to the vein. Since the gold becomes finer as you go further downstream, searching for gold nuggets and specimens closer to the site of the decomposed vein is going to be more productive than going many miles downstream would be.

One more:

> *"Connor Creek was known for its fine specimens of coarse gold. The total production from both placer and quartz mining is estimated at*

$1,250,000. The Connor Creek quartz mine was among the heavy producers. A twenty-stamp mill crushed the ore for a number of years. In the mine were blocks of ore so hard they were piled to one side. Through curiosity one block was broken and, as the miners said, "It was lousy with gold." Thirty thousand dollars was taken from four tons of the hard rock."

Oregon's Golden Years by Miles F. Potter

Always look for any specific mention of the richness of ores. The term "free gold" or "free milling" is worth paying special attention to. It refers to an ore that is rich enough that it can be processed on-site by crushing. Miners would use arrastras, stamp mills, or other crude methods to extract the gold from quartz or other host rock. Any ore that is rich enough to have visible gold can likely be found with a metal detector. Searching old waste rock piles in the vicinity of abandoned lode mining operations can be productive if the ores were of sufficient richness.

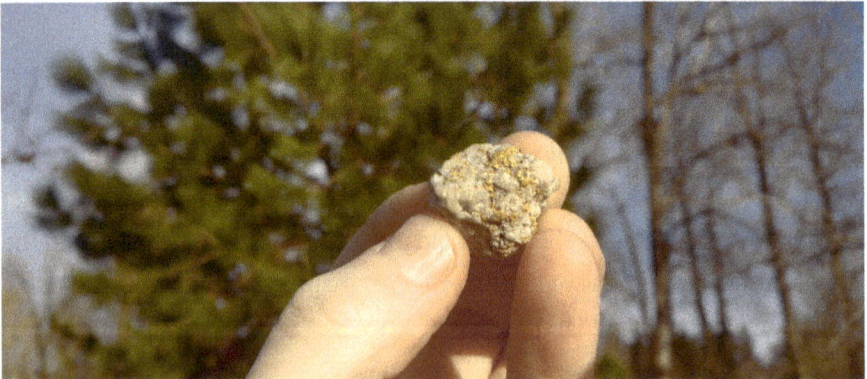

Quartz with visible gold can be found around old hard rock mines. Detecting the surrounding areas can result it nice specimens like this. Always pay attention whenever "free gold" or "free-milling gold" is mentioned in old literature.

Land Status (Finding Ground to Legally Prospect)

Truth be told, finding areas where gold nuggets might potentially be found is the easy part of research. Using the resources mentioned above, you will be able to locate plenty of areas that should pique your interest. Now the real challenge begins...

Much of the ground that you WANT to go metal detecting will be off-limits to you! This will vary widely depending on where you are, but its something I have experienced in every state I have tried to metal detect for gold. **MOST** of the best nugget hunting ground is not open for prospecting.

Every square foot of land in the United States is owned/managed by someone. Whether that is private lands owned by an individual, public lands managed by the BLM or Forest Service, lands managed by the National Park Service, Indian Reservations, or other types of land designation, you need to know where you are and if you are legally allowed to metal detect there. Let's take a look at some of the main types of land that you are going to encounter:

- **Private Lands:** Respecting private property rights is the foundation of ethical and legal prospecting. Private lands are owned by individuals or entities, and prospecting on such properties without proper authorization is strictly prohibited and can lead to trespassing charges. Private lands offer some of the best gold prospecting and metal detecting opportunities today, but it is vital to research land ownership records and obtain written permission from the landowner before engaging in any prospecting activities on private lands.

- **National Parks:** The beauty of National Parks attracts millions of visitors each year, but these areas are under strict conservation management to preserve their ecological integrity. Gold prospecting is typically not allowed in National Parks, as it could disrupt sensitive ecosystems and cultural resources. The only exception that I am aware of is Wrangell-St. Elias National Park in Alaska allows some very minimal gold panning, but metal detecting is still now allowed. Generally speaking, the National Parks are off-limits and you'll need to look elsewhere.

· **National Recreation Areas:** There are varying rules and regulations for National Recreation Areas, and you should be extra careful to read and understand exactly what the law allows for each specific area. For example, Whiskeytown National Recreation Area allows panning, but no sieves, classifiers, picks, shovels or tools of any kind and absolutely no metal detecting. Fines are severe for those who ignore the rules. Unfortunately, the rules in different areas often seem to be arbitrary and at the whim of whoever is in charge at any given time. Rules seem to only get more restrictive over time. As with National Parks, be very cautious and understand the rules to avoid serious fines or worse.

· **Other Special Land Designations:** Various other types of land designations, such as Wilderness Areas and Wildlife Refuges, may have specific rules and restrictions regarding prospecting activities. These designations exist to safeguard natural habitats and ensure sustainable land use. Prospectors will need to consult with relevant agencies and obtain the necessary permits or permissions if prospecting is allowed within these areas. Most of the time, metal detecting will be prohibited in these areas.

- **State Lands:** Again, the rules about prospecting on state lands will vary from state to state, so it will require some research to determine the legality of metal detecting. Some states are surprisingly strict about limiting casual prospecting on state lands. Do not mistake state land for federal land, as the management and enforcement is completely different.

- **Indian Reservations:** Indian Reservations are sovereign lands governed by Native American tribes. These lands are subject to distinct laws and regulations, which may vary from state and federal laws. Prospecting on Indian Reservations without explicit approval from the tribal authorities is a serious offense and can result in significant legal consequences. Prior to any prospecting activity, it is imperative to contact the relevant tribal government and seek their consent and guidance. I know of some very rich mining areas on Indian Reservation land that I would love to metal detect, but as a non-tribal member, I have never had any luck acquiring permission.

- **Federal Lands (BLM and Forest Service):** The vast majority of public lands in the West are managed by the BLM and USFS. Many of the most mineral rich states like Arizona, California, Idaho, Oregon and Nevada have lots of open ground that you can prospect on.

These quotes come directly from the Forest Service website:

"It is Forest Service policy that the recreational use of metal detectors and the collection of rocks and mineral samples are allowed on the National Forests. Generally, most of the National Forests are open to recreational mineral and rock collecting, gold panning and prospecting using a metal detector. This low impact, casual activity usually does not require any authorization."

"Using a metal detector to locate gold or other mineral deposits is an allowed activity under the General Mining Laws..."

So as a general rule, it is perfectly legal for the casual prospector to venture out onto public lands and dig for gold. There are mining laws that have protected this practice since the days of the Gold Rush, and those same laws are still in place today.

For most gold detectorists, these public lands provide the best opportunities to find open ground to find gold nuggets. There are thousands of square miles that you can legally prospect for gold on public lands. Your biggest challenge will be finding the open areas where:

1. The land is open for metal detecting **AND...**
2. There is a high likelihood that nuggets are present **AND...**
3. If on public land, the land is not already claimed.

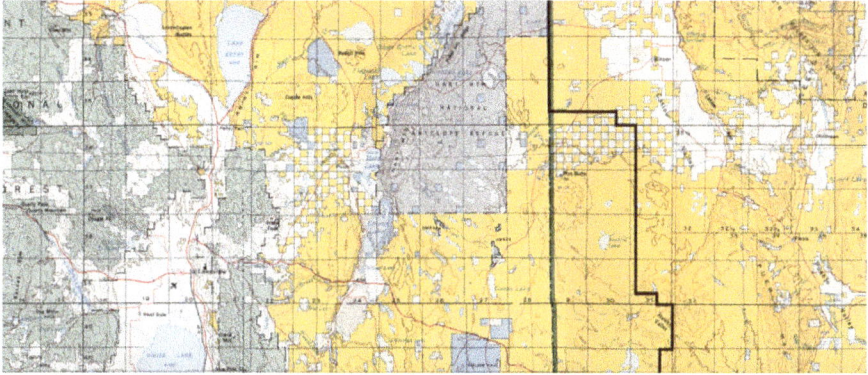

It's the responsibility of every gold prospector to understand how to research land status to determine what ground is open to them for prospecting. Understanding how to read a map and locate public land is important. There are vast amounts of public land that are open to legally prospect. Other areas like private land, state managed lands, wildlife refuges or actively claimed land may be off-limits to you.

Mining Claims

You've likely heard the terms "claim jumper" or "high grader" before, but you may not really understand what it is or exactly how a claim works. In my experience, concerns about mining claims, or the fear of accidentally being a "claim jumper" is one of the biggest deterrents for new prospectors.

First let me point out that you **do not need a mining claim to prospect for gold.** I have never owned a claim, and many prospectors I know have also never owned a claim.

A mining claim is a legal right granted to an individual or a company by the government to explore, mine, and extract valuable minerals or resources from a designated area of public land. Mining claims are typically associated with the exploration and extraction of minerals like gold, silver, copper, coal, and other valuable substances.

In the United States, mining claims are governed by the General Mining Law of 1872, which was passed to encourage the exploration and development of mineral resources on federal lands. The law allows individuals and entities to stake a claim on federal lands that are open to mineral entry. This process grants them exclusive rights to explore and develop the minerals within the defined claim boundaries.

To obtain a mining claim, the claimant must locate a specific area of land that is open to mineral entry and contains the desired minerals. The claimant then must physically stake and mark the boundaries of the claim on the ground, typically with posts or markers, and file the appropriate paperwork with the Bureau of Land Management (BLM) or other relevant federal or state agencies.

By staking a mining claim, the claimant gains the right to explore for minerals and develop mining operations within the claim boundaries. This right includes the extraction and sale of minerals found within the claim area. **However, it is important to note that mining claims do not grant ownership of the land itself. The land remains under federal management, and the claimant's rights are limited to the minerals and resources they discover and extract.**

To maintain the validity of a mining claim, claimants must fulfill certain requirements, including performing annual assessment work or making cash payments to the government. Failure to meet these requirements can result in the claim being forfeited and becoming open to other prospectors once again.

Mining claims play a significant role in mineral exploration and development, but they also create a lot of confusion and fear. Even experienced gold prospectors don't always understand the details of how mining claims work.

For beginners, I find that very few of them have any intention to trespass on someones mining claim. This concern will often deter them from prospecting at all out of fear that they might be on someones claim. So how do we determine which lands are claimed and which ones aren't?

Researching Claims and Finding Unclaimed Ground

Determining if a section of land has a mining claim on it involves conducting research to check the public records and databases that track mining claims.

The presence of a claim marker on the land is not a good indicator of the claim status. Claim markers can get knocked down, stolen, or otherwise removed from a site. This does not mean that the claim is inactive. In contrast, old claim markers may still be standing from years ago... even after the claim is abandoned. To be certain of claim status, you need to do the research.

Here are the steps you can follow to research mining claims on a specific piece of land:

1. **Identify the Location:** First, you need to know the exact location of the land you are interested in researching. This typically involves having the legal description of the property, including the township, range, section, and meridian.

2. **Bureau of Land Management Records:** The Bureau of Land Management in the United States is responsible for managing public lands and mining claims. You can start your research by visiting the BLM's website (**https://www.blm.gov/**) and using their online tools to search for mining claims. They provide access to the LR2000 system, which is a database that contains information on federal mining claims. Go to the LR2000 website (**https://www.blm.gov/services/national-lr2000**). Use the search tools to input the location details or other relevant information.

Review the mining claims records for the specified area. You can obtain information about active claims, claimants, claim status, and more.

3. **County Recorder's Office:** Mining claims are also be recorded at the county level. Contact the county recorder's office for the county where the land is located. They may have records of mining claims, including location notices and mining claim deeds.

4. **State Agencies:** In some cases, state agencies may also maintain records of mining claims within their jurisdiction. Check with the relevant state agency responsible for mining or natural resources for additional information.

In known gold-bearing areas, it is common to find that the area you are interested in once had historical mining claims on the land, but there is no longer active an claim. This means that the ground is now open to prospect.

It's crucial to approach this research carefully. If you are new to this process, it may be beneficial to seek advice from more experienced miner. I have spoken with geologists at the BLM who were very helpful as well, particularly with how to navigate the LR2000 website. Mining claim records can be complex, but once you learn the process it is not too difficult to understand.

Interacting with Landowners & Claimants to Obtain Permission for Access

Most of the **best** areas to metal detect for gold are not currently open or accessible for prospecting. Often times, the end result of your mining claim research will indicate that the area that you wanted to prospect is already claimed. In other instances, the land is privately owned and not accessible to the public.

If this is the case, don't get discouraged! **Some of the best days I've ever had nugget hunting have been on private land.** Rather than hunting ground that has been hammered by other prospectors, the extra work required to gain access to private land helped me discover nugget patches that few prospectors have had the opportunity to find.

Approaching a landowner to request permission to go metal detecting on their land requires courtesy, respect, and a well-thought-out approach. Here are some tips for making a successful request:

- **Research the Landowner:** Try to gather information about the landowner, such as their name, contact information, and any relevant background details. This may be obvious if there is a house adjacent to the land, but in some instances you will need to do more research. This information through public records or by asking local residents. There are now many Land Ownership apps now that will show this information right on your phone. The app I use is called onX.

- **Be Respectful and Ask:** Approach the landowner with a polite and respectful attitude. Address them with respect and let them know your intentions. Nowadays, people are pretty wary of strangers on their doorstep. Get to the point. Introduce yourself and explaining your purpose for contacting them. Mention your interest in metal detecting and your desire to do so on their property.

- **Share Your Experience and Knowledge:** There's a good possibility that the landowner will have no idea that there could even be gold on their property. This can be a good opportunity to teach them a little bit about the mining history of the area. Arouse their curiosity with the mining activity that once took place in the area.

- **Be Prepared to Alleviate Their Concerns:** I try to anticipate any concerns that the landowner might have. One big one is that you will **FILL YOUR HOLES** and leave the land as good as you found it.

- **Offer Compensation:** Depending on the direction of the conversation, you may consider offering compensation for their permission. This could be a share of any gold you find, a fee, or another mutually agreeable arrangement. Of course I prefer to keep the gold myself, but a modest access fee might be reasonable depending on how much potential the land has.

- **Respect Their Decision:** Regardless of their decision, whether they grant or deny permission, respect their choice. If they refuse permission, thank them for their time and consideration. A private land owner has no obligation to let you enter their land, so if they say no, respect that decision.

- **Follow Up:** Even if you don't gain access, consider following up with landowners. I've had lots of folks tell me "No," only to later grant me access weeks or months later when I've made a second visit. The success of this depends entirely on the above point. Be respectful even when they say no. It may pay off when you try again later.

- **Written Agreement:** If the landowner grants permission, it's a good practice to send them a written agreement outlining the basic terms and conditions of your access. This can help prevent misunderstandings in the future. Keep it simple through, you don't want to scare a landowner with a bunch of paperwork that reads like a legal document.

Remember that every landowner is different, and their decision may be influenced by various factors, including their personal experiences, property values, and concerns about liability. Approach the conversation with patience and a willingness to negotiate if necessary. Building a positive and respectful relationship with the landowner can lead to access to areas that hold amazing potential for prospecting.

Everything above can also be said about claim holders as well. You'd be surprised how often a claimant will grant you access to prospect on their claim if you just ask. Usually I do a handshake agreement with them and offer to give them a percentage of the gold that I find when I am prospecting.

Just as with a private landowner, this can take some time to build a relationship. Honesty and integrity will get you far... if you don't hold to your word, you aren't honest about the gold that you are finding, or otherwise act "shady" then you can expect to lose access eventually. If everyone shares in your success you will discover that people will talk with their friends and neighbors, and new ground may open up to you.

Gold Deposits

Placer vs. Lode Gold

All gold sources can broadly be separated into two main types: Placer gold and lode gold deposits. These are two distinct types of gold deposits that differ in their geological origin, formation processes, and characteristics. Within these two categories, there are many subcategories which we will look at later in this chapter.

Metal detectors can be useful in locating gold at both of these general deposit types, though the techniques used to search for gold may vary depending on the site.

Here's a general breakdown of the differences between the placer and lode gold.

Lode Deposits

Lode deposits, also known as hard rock, vein, or ore deposits, originate from the source of the gold mineralization deep within the Earth's crust. These deposits form when hydrothermal fluids, often containing gold-bearing minerals, circulate through fractures, faults, and fissures in the rock. As the fluids cool and deposit minerals, including gold, they form veins or mineralized zones within the host rock.

Lode gold deposits are typically composed of quartz veins or other mineralized structures that contain gold-bearing minerals. The gold in lode deposits is usually more interconnected with the host rock and can be disseminated throughout the vein or concentrated in specific sections. Lode deposits can also contain other valuable minerals and metals associated with the hydrothermal mineralization process.

I don't recommend going into underground mines unless you have the proper training. Most of them have been abandoned for decades or centuries now, and there are a myriad of dangers.

Lode deposits are often concentrated in specific geological settings. They are more commonly found in regions with a history of tectonic activity, volcanic processes, and the formation of mineralizing hydrothermal fluids.

Large-scale lode mining involves more complex and intensive methods. Depending on the depth and extent of the deposit, methods such as underground mining (tunnels and shafts) and open-pit mining might be used to extract the gold-bearing ore. Crushing, grinding, and chemical processing are often required to extract the gold from the host rock. However, metal detectors can be used at lode mines to detect gold in many ways, ranging from locating veins directly in the rock, or more commonly by searching old dump piles adjacent to lode mines in search of gold bearing "float" and high-grade specimen gold that was discarded in the waste piles.

Gold-bearing hydrothermal fluids can cause alteration of the host rocks, leading to the formation of minerals such as iron oxides, silicates, and sulfides. The alteration processes can contribute to the development of distinctive rock formations and mineral assemblages that might be associated with gold-bearing areas.

Gold itself might not directly contribute to the red color of the soil, but the processes that lead to gold enrichment in a particular area can also contribute to the alteration of rocks and the formation of iron oxides. Secondary enrichment involves the leaching of gold from its original source and its redeposition in concentrated form, often resulting in altered rock formations.

Hydrothermal gold deposits are generally the most important for the metal detectorist because they have the greatest potential to produce large detectable gold. Many other ore deposits that are mined around the world are very productive for large-scale mining, but are essentially worthless to the detectorist due to the extra small gold that they produce.

Placer Deposits

Placer deposits are formed through the erosion and weathering of primary gold-bearing rocks (lode deposits). Over time, the gold is released from these rocks due to natural processes like weathering, erosion, and chemical dissolution. The liberated gold particles are then transported by water, such as rivers and streams, and eventually settle in areas where the water slows down, like riverbeds, stream channels, and beaches.

Unlike lode gold that will often be rough textured and attached to host rock, placer gold is usually found as particles, flakes, or nuggets that have been weathered and rounded by the action of water. The size of the gold particles can vary widely, from very small grains to larger nuggets. Placer deposits are often found in riverbeds, floodplains, alluvial fans, and coastal areas.

Placer mining involves techniques such as panning, sluicing, dredging, and hydraulic mining. These methods rely on the gravity separation of gold from the surrounding gravel and sediment.

Early placer miners found a lot of gold, but they never found it all. Finding old mining sites like this and searching them with metal detectors can be very productive.

Generally speaking, placer gold is easier to recover using basic prospecting methods, so it's more commonly searched for by casual prospectors. Many placers produce good sized gold particles, ranging from "pickers" on up to nuggets that can easily be located with a metal detector. These are the most important gold deposits for most electronic prospectors.

Placer deposits are more widely distributed geographically and can travel great distances through the process of erosion. Tiny particles of gold can travel hundreds of miles from its original lode source. They often occur in areas where water has played a significant role in transporting and depositing gold particles.

Types of Gold Placers

Weathering of gold from its lode source produces placers, which can deposit in a variety of different ways. These placer deposits are classified into several different types. It's worth noting that the various processes of weathering and erosion can result in some overlap within these types, but broadly understanding the ways that gold accumulates into concentrated sources is incredibly important if you want to be a successful prospector.

IDEALIZED CROSS SECTION SHOWING FORMATION OF COMMON PLACER GOLD DEPOSITS.

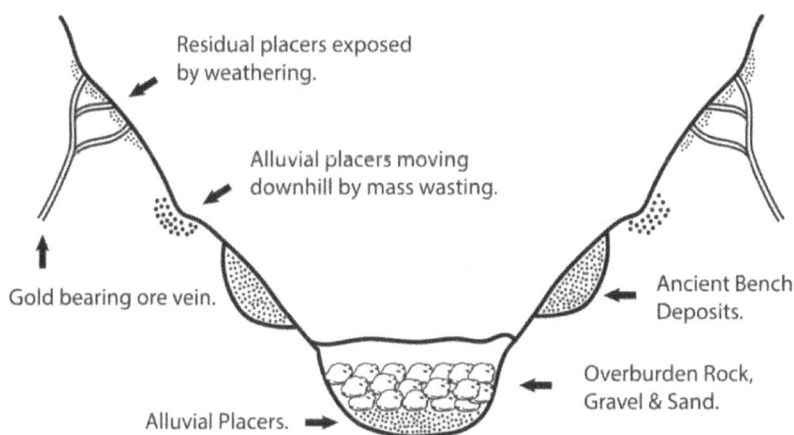

Residual placers exposed by weathering.

Alluvial placers moving downhill by mass wasting.

Gold bearing ore vein.

Ancient Bench Deposits.

Overburden Rock, Gravel & Sand.

Alluvial Placers.

This example shows some of the more common types of gold deposits that you might encounter. The gold bearing vein provides the source of gold here, but beyond the detectable depth of your detector, the lode deposits are mostly out of reach. It is the results of weathering and erosion over millions of years that expose and concentrate the gold in deposits that you can locate with your metal detector.

Alluvial Deposits

An alluvial gold deposit is a type of placer deposit where gold particles and nuggets are eroded from their source rock, transported by water, and then deposited in areas like riverbeds, stream channels, and floodplains, where the water's flow slows down. These deposits make up a large percentage of the placer gold found throughout the Western U.S., and were the first areas that were generally exploited by the early miners. Alluvial deposits can be refreshed by major flooding event and annual spring runoff, but finding areas of accumulated gravels that have not been mined will generally be much more productive.

Eluvial Deposits

Eluvial deposits are often referred to as hillside deposits. The are usually found near the surface where natural erosion over time has weathered gold out of the bedrock, leaving it detached from the host rock. Prospectors and miners can access them through surface excavation or shallow digging. They are often located on hillsides, terraces, or slopes. Eluvial deposits are often found very near the site of exposure, but over time they will creep down the hillside and find their way into concentrations in washes and arroyos. Eluvial deposits hold excellent potential for metal detectorists.

Residual Deposits

As hillside gold deposits erode and form secondary deposits, they will concentrate into what are known as residual deposits. This gold hasn't moved far, and will often still be coarse and angular shaped with quartz matrix still attached. The discovery of a rich residual prospect can lead a prospector to an eluvial deposit, and possibly even a lode gold source if the vein is still present in the ground.

Bajada Deposits

Bajada gold deposits are typically found in arid or desert regions, specifically on the alluvial fans that form at the base of mountains or hills. Bajadas are broad, gently sloping or fan-shaped land forms composed of sediment and alluvial material that have been transported and deposited by intermittent streams and flash floods. Bajada deposits can be productive for metal detecting, but often the gold is too deep with overburden to be detected effectively.

Glacial Deposits

These gold deposits are the result of past glacial movement where to gold was physically transported across the landscape. Glacial deposits occur all around the globe in areas where glaciers advanced down and pushed rock and gravel with them. Glaciers can grind and crush the rocks and minerals they carry, including gold-bearing quartz veins or other host rocks. This mechanical action can liberate gold particles from their original matrix. These deposits are widespread and cover vast landscapes all across the globe. One thing that is consistent with glacial deposits is that they are comprised of very small gold particles, making them of little interest for metal detecting.

Eolian Deposits

These are highly localized concentrations of gold which have been formed when winds blow away lighter materials, thus concentrating the heavy materials in-situ. Eolian deposits are most common if flat, windblown desert areas like Australia and the American Southwest. These are some of the best gold deposits for detectorists to focus their attention. Nuggets will be close to the surface and easily detected.

Beach Placers

It's not uncommon for gold particles to concentrate on beaches. The most famous beach placers were those at Nome, Alaska, but other rich concentrations have been found in other areas of Alaska, Washington, Oregon and California. While these can be quite rich, the gold is very small particles and of little interest to the detectorist.

Bench Placers (Ancient Rivers)

Bench gold deposits, often referred to as bench placers, are a type of placer gold deposit that is typically found on the terraces or benches of river valleys, particularly in mountainous or hilly regions. These deposits are associated with the ancient river systems and processes that once transported and concentrated gold in the past. These are ancient alluvial deposits that have been left "high and dry" as the river cuts down. In some areas, such as the California Mother Lode, the uplift of the mountains also plays a part in raising up these ancient gravel beds. These ancient river channels may be a few feet above the current river level, or they may be *thousands of feet* above the current water level. Always keep an eye out for smooth, water-worn rock that are seem out of place.

General Observations: Indicators of Gold Bearing Areas

When I first started gold prospecting, I had this idea that I would become a master geologist. I figured if I understood the rock types and geological conditions where gold is commonly found, I would have a leg-up on the competition and finding gold would be easy.

A basic understanding of geology is certainly a good skill, but I quickly learned that simply being able to identify a type of rock wasn't exactly enough to put gold in your poke. What I eventually determined was that a even a college degree in Geology was no guarantee that you would be able to find gold.

The real secret is to be observant. When you are in an area that is known to contain gold, slow down and pay attention to what is around you. As time goes by and you prospect in different locations, you will start to notice similarities in the ground conditions. I know a lot of very good prospectors who might fail a the most basic Geology 101 test, but they know "good ground" when they see it.

"Gold Rides and Iron Horse"

Dark red colored soils often result from the presence of iron oxides, which give the soil its characteristic red color. The presence of iron oxides in the soil is due to a combination of weathering processes and the particular mineralogy of the parent rocks. Gold is commonly associated with areas with iron mineralization.

The process of soil formation involves the breakdown of rocks and minerals through physical, chemical, and biological processes. In areas with a humid climate, where water is abundant, these processes can lead to the leaching of many minerals from the soil, leaving behind iron oxides that are relatively insoluble and resistant to further weathering. Over time, these iron oxides accumulate and give the soil its reddish color, although these soils can actually have a wide array of coloration ranging from yellow, orange to deep red and purple.

While red soils themselves are not a direct indicator of gold nuggets, they can be indicative of geological processes that could lead to the presence of gold deposits. A wide variety of gold deposits can be associated with iron, so always be observant and keep an eye out.

Specific Rock Types

While you don't need to be an experienced geologist to be a successful gold prospector, having a basic understanding of rock types will certainly help you in your search for gold. There are some types of rock that have gold and some that don't, so knowing now to identify granite, greenstone, slate, schist, quartz and other rock types can help you identify areas with a higher likelihood of having gold deposits.

Always pay close attention when researching old mining reports. They will usually tell you exactly what type of rock the gold deposits in a certain area are associated with.

Having mentioned some of the common rock types associated with gold deposits, I will say that I find this information to be only slightly important in regards to becoming a successful gold hunter. Certainly a basic understanding of geology and the ability to spot certain geological conditions can be beneficial, but the "book knowledge" will only get you so far. Being observant to your surroundings and noticing trends and patterns associated with areas that produce gold is much more valuable.

A Special Word about Quartz

Quartz is a crystalline mineral comprised of silica (silicon dioxide). It is a hard mineral that is commonly associated with gold. Gold veins often form directly within quartz, and in some areas its common for detectorists to find gold nuggets that still have quartz attached to them. In some instances, specimens area found that are mostly quartz that will show gold veins running through them.

The relationship between quartz and gold is clear. Yet over the years, I have heard a lot of prospectors who seem to give too much attention to quartz. *The presence of quartz by itself is actually a fairly poor indicator for gold.*

Silica is one of the most abundant minerals in the Earth's crust. There are lots of places where you can go out and find pieces of quartz far from any existing gold deposits.

Quartz in and of itself does not mean gold is near. Just because gold can occur in conjunction with quartz doesn't mean that quartz by itself holds much interest.

Historical Mining Activity

Identifying Historic Mining

Learning to identify the signs of historic mining activity is one of the best "shortcuts" to finding gold-bearing areas. There are many different indicators that can lead you to areas where the old-timers used to dig for gold. These same areas will still produce gold today, and are often the best areas to search for nuggets with your metal detector.

The indicators of past mining activity can be as subtle as a small pile of rocks, or as obvious as a giant open-pit mine. Let's take a look at some of the more common signs of past mining activity.

Bucket Dredge Tailings

Bucketline dredge tailings are the remnants resulting from the operation of bucketline dredges, large machines used for extracting minerals from alluvial deposits like riverbeds. These tailings form as the discarded materials once valuable minerals, such as gold, have been extracted from the sediments.

Bucket dredges like this one in Alaska left behind expansive tailing piles. Large nuggets would be rejected by the screens and discarded in these piles.

The dredge's buckets scoop up sediment, conveying it for processing on the dredge to recover minerals. The remaining material, which includes fine sands, silt, clay, rocks and boulders, constitutes the tailings. Lighter material that has become exposed is often carried away by erosion, leaving distinctive sediment patterns comprised mostly of larger rocks.

Due to the amount of material that they processed, dredges were often inefficient at gold recovery. A decent amount of gold was not captured and it would find its way back into the tailing piles. Additionally, dredges were set up to screen out larger rocks to prevent them from clogging up the sluices inside the dredge. As a result, large nuggets and gold/quartz specimens would be kicked out the back of the dredge.

Dredge tailings are challenging to hunt due to the amount of trash and hot rocks that can be found in among the gravel, but they also hold great potential for metal detecting. Hunting them require a great amount of patience, but some dredge tailing piles hide a lot of gold. Some of my biggest nuggets have been dug from old dredge tailings.

Most dredge tailings aren't hard to find. This is an aerial photo of the lower Yuba River just east of Yuba City, California. These tailings are comprised of gravel and large rocks that cover an area nearly 2 miles wide and over 10 miles long. © Google Maps, 2024.

Small Placer Mining Activity

Identifying rock piles that indicate past placer mining activity involves recognizing certain characteristics that are often associated with historical placer mining operations. Placer mining often takes place near water bodies such as rivers and creeks. Also consider that the creeks may be seasonally dry, and the placer mining took place during as short time in the spring when water was present. Look for rock piles along the banks of these areas or in areas where water flow was diverted for mining purposes.

Many historic placer mining operations were not mechanized. They generally involved manually sorting through sediment with picks and shovels. This resulted in distinctive piles of rocks or gravels that were separated from the finer materials. Look for rocks that appear to be sorted or piled together, potentially different from the surrounding natural geology. These large rocks were stacked to the side as the miners dug down toward bedrock in search of gold.

Much of the historic mining activity involved little more than shovels, pans and sluice boxes. These small operations never found all the gold, and surely left a few nuggets behind.

The sluice boxes that were built to process the gravels are now rotted away and gone, but be on the lookout of an abundance of old iron trash like square nails, spikes, or strapping material. This can be a good indicator.

When identifying rock piles that indicate past placer mining activity, a combination of careful observation, research, and an understanding of mining techniques and geological context can help you locate these historical sites.

Hydraulic Mines (Ground Sluicing)

Hydraulic mining was a type of operation that used water under high pressure to wash away gold-bearing material to be run through a sluice box. There are probably thousands of old hydraulic "pits" scattered throughout the West.

These are great spots to find gold nuggets, but they can be difficult to hunt with a detector. Some of them are so large, that figuring out just where the best place to hunt can be very difficult, but I'll provide a few tips that will help you.

The monitors, or "water cannons" that the miners used were set up in strategic locations so that they could wash the ground around them. At first glance it might seem impossible to know where they were set up, but careful evaluation of the ground around you can help you figure it out.

Monitors were often perched up on a piece of unmined ground. Look for a small plateau of ground that wasn't washed away. Closer inspection will often reveal lots of iron rubbish on the ground around it. Once you locate the location of the monitors, you can visualize how the mine was set up. You can see the areas were the water washed, and the areas where the water wasn't able to reach.

Hydraulic mining was done all throughout the world. Huge water cannons were used to break up gravel, which would then run through sluices to capture the gold. They were highly effective in their ability to move tons of material during the early days, but they were not always efficient. Gold was left behind.

You will often notice spots where more rocks are piled up that appear to be flat shaped or perhaps darker, heavier stones. Sometimes they will be on the farther ends of the pits, where the water pressure was too weak to move them. The water may have been too weak to move heavier gold nuggets as well. This is a good area to search with your metal detector.

The miners set up sluice boxes down in the gulleys to process all the material they were washing. They were usually not very efficient, and considerable gold was lost. Sometimes the gold was lost when riffles overloaded and gold blew out of the sluice, completely missed. Work the bottoms carefully with your detector.

Look for jagged bedrock that could potentially trap a gold nugget. If the water pressure wasn't strong enough, the water would actually help to settle a gold nugget was deep down into those cracks. Yet another good spot to search.

Prospectors know all too well about that challenges of clay, and how it will trap gold if it isn't broke up thoroughly. Well, the hydraulic miners had this same problem. The hydraulic operations would break out clay chunks that contained gold. If they weren't carefully washed, they would lock up gold. These clay areas can be worth checking.

Some hydraulic pits are very trashy. Unfortunately, they seems to attract every target shooter within a 10 mile radius! If there is a lot of trash, don't give up. Use a metal detector with good discrimination and keep hunting, only digging select targets. Have perseverance and you may find some gold nuggets among the trash, but sometimes the bullets are just too much, and it's a lost cause.

Some of the old hydraulic mining pits employed dozens of men and covered hundreds of acres. These were major mining operations and obviously they were finding a lot of gold.

There are also small hydraulic operations that are only an acre or less in size. They used just a small amount of water from a creek or small man-made reservoir, and may be overgrown with brush and trees now. Many of them have never been hunted with a modern metal detector because they have been overlooked completely. It takes a keen eye to spot them.

As always, research is a big part of finding hydraulic pits. They are productive places to metal detect. I hunt them all, large and small. They all contain gold, although not always in the form of large nuggets. Dust, flakes, small nuggets, huge nuggets... you never know what you'll find when hunting old pits.

Drywasher Piles

Gold prospectors in arid regions are limited in the ways that they can recover gold. Many of the methods that work elsewhere are not feasible in the desert. Water is the basic requirement for a wide variety of placer mining methods. Panning, sluicing, dredging, high banking, and even using a simple rocker box all require some water.

Yet, in many parts of the world (and here in the USA in places like Arizona, Nevada, New Mexico and Southern California) the gold deposits are too far away from water to be worked effectively.

A device known as a drywasher (also sometimes called a dry blower or Mexican jig) was the tool of choice for the early desert miner. They were the perfect piece of mining equipment for the individual miner to work isolated desert gold placers far from any existing water. Rather than needing water like so most other methods, a drywasher uses a combination of vibration and puffs of air to agitate and separate gold from gravels. Miners simply shoveled dry dirt into the machine, and chunky gold flakes and nuggets could be recovered from the desert dirt.

A considerable amount of gold was missed by these old drywashers. Slightly damp soils might prevent the gold from separating out from the dirt, and specimens of gold with quartz might simply tumble through the machine because the specific gravity was too low. Screens that were designed to keep large rocks out of the machine would also separate out a large nugget. As a result, drywasher tailing piles can still contain nuggets that were missed by the old-timers.

As important as the drywashers were for opening up areas that wouldn't otherwise be economically viable to mine, they had one big disadvantage. They weren't all that efficient. A considerable amount of gold was missed by these old drywashers.

The early miners could still make it worth their while to mine if an area was rich enough, but no matter how well they did, they were still losing some gold in their tailing piles. We know that these old dry mining operations missed some gold, so they are the perfect place for you to come back to and seek out the gold that was missed. And the tailing piles left behind are the best indication of these early operations.

It might be surprising to some that a trained eye can still spot an old drywasher operation from 100+ years ago. They are actually pretty easy to located if you know what you are looking for. There will be unusual piles of rocks and gravels, often alongside a dry creek bed or gulley. Rocks will often be sorted in similar sizes and look a bit out of place from their surroundings. Larger tailing piles can often be seen using Google Earth and similar aerial imagery.

You have to ask yourself, why would this rock pile be here? If you are in an area that is known historically for gold mining, then you can bet that you've found an old drywasher pile. Anywhere with these piles is a tell-tale sign that miners found gold here.

Now is where we use modern technology to our advantage. Those old drywashers missed some nice nuggets that can be easily located with a good metal detector. Swing your coil slowly and deliberately over the gravel piles, taking extra care to go over every bit of the pile and extend your search several feet to the sides too. Be thorough.

When detecting drywash tailings, I recommend bringing along a sturdy rake. After scanning the top of a pile, take off about 2 inches of gravel from the top and scan it again. Repeat this process throughout the pile, each time doing a slow and deliberate search of the newly exposed pile. This method will often turn up very small nuggets that were out of reach before. This is particularly effective if another detectorist has already searched the area. They may have come in and cleaned out the surface nuggets, but a little extra effort with your rake can lead to a lot more finds.

The idea of detecting these old piles is certainly not a new idea. In fact, detectorists have been doing it for as long as good gold detectors have been available. This makes the rake-and-detect trick even more important.

One other thing that I would recommend is to extend your search off of the piles and explore the surrounding hills, even if there is no evidence that would indicate past mining efforts. Some might call this patch hunting. The nearby tailing piles are proof that gold occurs in the area, so now you extend your search to nearby gulches and washes that may have been missed by the old-timers.

Hillside Pocket Digging

Pocket gold is different than what is typically found in most areas. It should not be confused with typical stream placer gold, which is a concentration of gold in a river or stream. This gold comes from potentially many different eroded lode sources.

Pocket gold is more closely associated with lode gold, but most of these deposits differ because in most cases the gold is extremely localized. Whereas much of the lode gold is mined out of a quartz vein that may travel great distances, pockets are generally gold enrichments found near the surface. Most of them are SMALL. In some cases, ALL of the gold will be localized in a small area of only a few square yards.

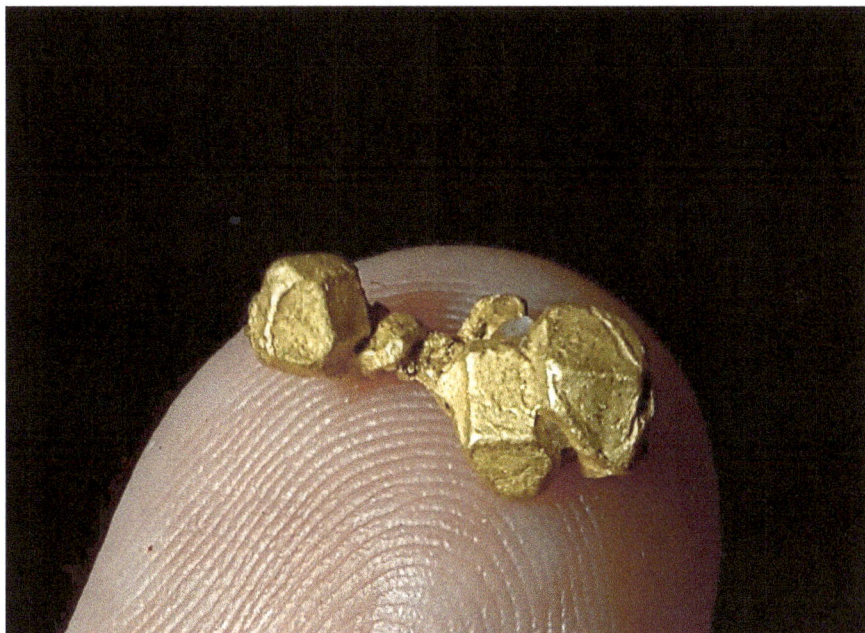

Gold like this is one of the "perks" of hunting hillsides and other areas where the gold has not become smooth or water worn. This geometric little gold crystal clearly hasn't been eroded and has an incredible shape. A piece like this might bring ten or twenty times the spot price of gold to a serious collector.

In many ways, hunting for pocket gold is a true treasure hunt, where the final result has the potential for great discoveries. As most gold prospectors know, placer mining using basic tools may average a gram of gold after a day of hard work, but without the use of mechanized equipment it is very hard for a casual prospector to recover large concentrations of gold nowadays.

Many hillside pocket diggings are exploratory, and don't necessarily indicate that any gold was actually found in the area. A miner might have had a hunch that there was gold there, spent a day or two digging and then moved on. Just seeing some old workings is no guarantee that gold was found there, but it's certainly worth spending a little time investigating with your detector.

Lode Mines and Ore Dumps

When a miner discovered a rich gold outcrop and found that the more gold continued into the mountain, a lode mine would be developed. The size and scale of each mine varied, but many mines tunneled hundreds and even thousands of feet into the hillside following a gold vein. The ore would then be taken out of the mountain and processed.

Stamp mills like this were used to crush ore and extract gold from rock. Large mines would have them on-site, but many smaller mines would have to transport their ore to have it processed elsewhere. This was not a small undertaking, so miners would often "high-grade," only transporting the richest ore.

If the ore was free-milling, it would be crushed and the gold would be extracted. This was a very expensive process, and often **the ore needed to be very high-grade to be considered worthy of processing. For this reason there can often be ore found near old lode mines that was never processed and sometimes it contains gold.**

Scanning old ore dumps with a metal detector can be productive. Just remember, there were no "rules" on how to it was done back then, and not all of the mines were operated the same way. Some lode mines were very efficiently run and you may have a hard time finding a piece of ore with detectable gold. Other times, the miners were sloppy. They discarded pieces of high-grade ore with visible gold, and it can still be found in the waste rock piles. You never know what you will find until you look.

This is a good time to mention that it is never a good idea to enter an old mine. Be careful when detecting around old mines. There may be hidden shafts that are hidden in the brush or other dangers. People die every year from going underground in old mine shafts. They can collapse. They often contain hazardous gasses. There may be snakes, bats, spiders, and all kinds of nasty stuff in them. Unless you have the appropriate training and experience, NEVER enter an abandoned mine shaft.

Bulldozer Scrapes

A more modern indicator of gold mining activity is bulldozer scrapes. These are area where a bulldozer has been used to remove layers of earth to expose new gold bearing ground. It is common to see these in the desert, and the practice is used in combination with metal detectors. I've run across quite a few of these in Northern Nevada.

Once an area has been detected and all of the easily detectable gold is found, a bulldozer scrapes off a foot or two of material, exposing new ground that can be detected. The processes can be continued as long as there is still gold being found.

These can be excellent areas to find gold, but be aware that there are permitting processes required to do this sort of thing, and basically all areas that are actively being mined like this are on private lands or claimed land. Still, you can find older bulldozer scrapes on unclaimed land that were done years ago that still may produce a gold nugget or two. You'll be reworking ground that has already been detected, so go "slow and low" with your coil.

Metal Rubbish

A very general tip for when you are out detecting is to always be on the lookout for old rusty metal. This is an indicator that someone spent time in the area. There's a good chance that it was miners looking for gold.

If you are detecting old rusty cans, square nails, boot tacks, metal straps or anything else that might indicate that men were once working in the area then you are on the right track. They were there for a reason!

Some miners would keep those old tobacco tins to hold the gold they found. I'm still dreaming of someday finding one that is still packed with gold nuggets!

Techniques and Strategies for Gold Detecting

Setting up your Metal Detector (Read the Manual!)

Setting up your metal detector before you start using it should be a no-brainer, but I've had a surprising number of people ask me some incredibly simple questions about their new metal detector. Almost all of the time, my response of "Did you read the owner's manual?" is met with quiet confusion.

In this chapter, I'm going to discuss some of the techniques to increase your odds of success when gold detecting, including proper setup and settings. What I want to avoid is filling pages and pages with redundant information that is simply a rehash of information that you would find in your owner's manual. For many issues, the owner's manual will do a better job of this than I can, because them most detailed answers that are specifically suited to your model of metal detector will be found there.

Reading the owner's manual when learning to use your metal detector is important for many reasons. The owner's manual provides a comprehensive guide to understanding all the features, settings, and functions of your specific metal detector model. While the basic design and function of handheld metal detectors are similar, each specific detector model is different. You should learn and understand as much as you can before you even turn on your detector, as it will help shorten your learning curve. This knowledge ensures you can use the detector to its fullest potential and optimize its performance.

The manual will walk you through the setup process, including assembling the detector correctly and calibrating it for different ground conditions. Gold nuggets are almost always found in highly mineralized ground, which can create challenges for even the top-of-the-line gold detectors. Understanding proper setup will ensures that your detector is working as accurately and efficiently as possible for the conditions.

Understanding how to fine-tune the settings based on the environment and your preferences allows you to achieve the best performance from your metal detector, leading to improved target detection and fewer false signals. Your goal is to optimize your detectors ability to hear small nuggets and large, deep gold.

The manual will likely include essential safety instructions, such as how to handle the detector responsibly, proper battery usage, and guidelines to avoid hazardous situations while storing the device.

In case you encounter any issues or errors with the metal detector, the manual will typically have a troubleshooting section, helping you resolve common problems or help you to better understand how your detector operates without having to seek outside assistance.

Understanding Ground Balance and Mineralization

Ground balancing is a critical process in using a metal detector, especially in areas with varying soil mineralization. The Earth's soil contains various minerals that can interfere with a metal detector's ability to detect metal objects accurately. Ground balancing is a technique used to compensate for these soil mineralization effects and maintain the detector's sensitivity to metal targets while reducing false signals caused by the grounds natural variability.

When a metal detector is ground balanced, it essentially adjusts its internal settings to account for the mineral content in the soil. The process involves the detector analyzing the mineralization level of the ground beneath it and making appropriate adjustments to its circuitry. **The ability of a detector to ground balance effectively in mineralized ground is one of the main features that separates a good gold detector from a multi-purpose coin/relic detector.**

In some areas, "hot rocks" can be a real challenge. These are rocks with a high-iron content that will sound off like a metal target. There are some places where hot rocks are almost unbearable. Careful ground balancing can help your detector tune them out, although even the best settings won't always save you. In some areas, hot rocks can make for some extremely challenging detecting.

There are generally two main types of ground balancing:

1. **Manual Ground Balancing:** In this method, the user takes control of the ground balancing process. The metal detector provides a feature that allows the operator to manually adjust the ground balance setting. The user can manually "lock in" the ground settings and find the point where the detector becomes most stable and less affected by the ground's mineralization. With manual ground balance, it is very important to ground balance often, sometimes as frequently as every few seconds to achieve optimal performance.

2. **Automatic Ground Balancing:** Many modern metal detectors come with automatic ground balancing capabilities. These detectors use built-in algorithms and sensors to analyze the ground mineralization continuously. The detector then automatically adjusts its ground

balance setting as needed to maintain optimal performance without user intervention.

Ground balancing is crucial because, without it, the metal detector may become excessively sensitive to the minerals in the soil, leading to false signals, erratic behavior, and reduced detection depth for metal objects of interest. Upgrades in ground balancing capability is one of the main things that sets the modern gold detector apart from earlier detectors made decades ago. By properly ground balancing the metal detector, you ensure that it remains stable and responsive to real metal targets while eliminating chatter produced by mineralization in rocks, soils and any other non-metal items.

Use Lower Gain Settings at First

Using lower gain settings on your metal detector when starting out and gradually increasing the sensitivity as you gain familiarity is a good idea for several reasons:

1. Reduced False Signals: Lower gain settings help minimize false signals caused by ground mineralization, hot rocks, electromagnetic interference, or other environmental factors. As a beginner, it can be incredibly difficult to distinguish between genuine signals and noise. As you gain experience, its possible to learn to evaluate the tones of your detector to help differentiate the "good" from the "bad" signals. By starting with lower gain, you can focus on understanding the detector's responses to real targets without getting distracted by excessive false readings.
2. Learning the Detector's Behavior: Each metal detector behaves differently, and it takes time to understand its nuances and responses to various targets. This is true for different coil selections as well. Starting with lower gain allows you to get accustomed to the detector's behavior and develop a better sense of how it reacts to different metals and ground conditions.

3. Target Identification: With lower gain settings, the metal detector's signals are more stable and easier to interpret. You can better identify the type of metal and the depth of the target, helping you differentiate the metal targets.

4. Preventing Overwhelm: Gold detecting can be overwhelming for beginners, especially if they start with high sensitivity settings. The constant chatter of the ground and abundant trash targets can really be discouraging. Starting with lower settings provides a more manageable experience, making it easier for beginners to stay motivated and enjoy the process.

5. Protection from Electrical Interference: In areas with high electromagnetic interference, using high gain settings can lead to even more false signals and reduced performance. Starting with lower gain may be the only option to mitigate this issue and ensures better performance in challenging environments.

Don't fall into the trap of thinking that turning up all the knobs on your detector is going to give you better performance. This simply isn't how it works. You want your detector to be set up optimally for the ground conditions. Keeping your settings low help you understand the detector's behavior, identify targets more accurately, practice proper recovery techniques, and stay motivated as you gradually increase the sensitivity once you become more familiar with the device.

As you gain experience with your metal detector, you can then turn up the gain and experiment with other settings that may give you added depth.

Slow Down and Listen for the Faintest Signals

Most metal detectorists first started out by detecting for coins in the park. They are accustomed to mild soils and listening to big, booming target responses that you get from coins. They get accustomed to hunting rather quickly, covering a lot of ground and listening for those louder targets.

Nugget hunting is very different. Swinging the detector coil slowly when hunting for gold nuggets is absolutely essential in most circumstances. Unfortunately, there aren't very many big nuggets sitting close to the surface nowadays. If you are only digging those loud targets, you're likely to dig a bunch of nails, wire, shotgun pellets, and other metal rubbish, and your going to go right over the gold.

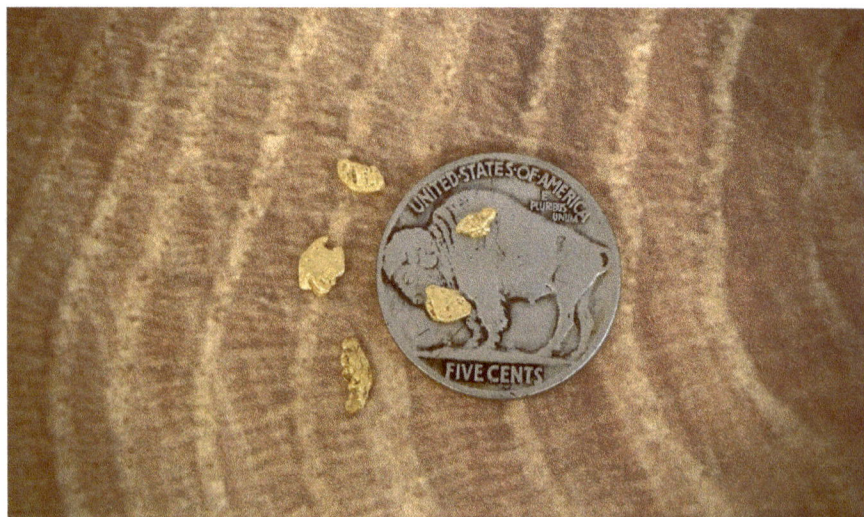

Gold nuggets, especially smaller ones or those embedded in mineralized soil, can be very challenging to hear in the ground. You almost never get a loud, booming target response from your detector. What you will usually get instead is just a tiny increase in the threshold hum. What you're listening for is consistent, repeatable changes in tone.

Swinging your coil too quickly will completely mask these tiny changes in threshold. When you swing the coil slowly, the metal detector has more time to analyze the ground's mineralization and pick up weak signals from smaller or deeper gold targets. Faster swinging will cause the detector to miss or overlook these faint signals.

The electromagnetic field produced by the coil needs time to penetrate the ground and return signals from deeper targets. Slow swinging allows the metal detector to provide a more accurate and defined response for detected targets. This enables the operator to distinguish between potential gold nuggets and other non-valuable metallic objects or mineral interference.

A controlled swing is critical for successful nugget detecting. Sweep your coil slowly from side-to-side, keeping the coil parallel to the ground. Maneuver methodically around rocks and shrubs. Avoid letting the coil lift up on the far side of each swing, as this severely reduces target detection depth.

Another added benefit of hunting slower is reduction in false signals. Moving your detect coil erratically will create excessive chatter that will become too frustrating to deal with.

You should also hunt slowly for the simple fact that you have done your research and you know that you are on good ground. If you have done all the research that we discussed in past chapters, you know that there is gold in the area. Slow down and hunt carefully and thoroughly.

Coil Options

Metal detector coils come in various sizes to suit different purposes and environments. The three primary coil sizes are:

Small Coils: These are typically the smallest coils and are designed for highly specific tasks. They are ideal for target separation in trashy areas or searching for small targets in places where larger coils might struggle. Small coils offer enhanced sensitivity on small gold, which makes them a favorite for many gold hunters. They are also suitable for detecting in tight spaces, such as between rocks or in dense undergrowth. However, they do have a reduced detection depth compared to larger coils.

Medium Coils: These are the most common coils that come bundled with metal detectors upon purchase. Medium-sized coils strike a balance between depth and sensitivity, making them versatile for general-purpose metal detecting. Medium coils offer a good compromise between target depth and target separation capabilities. I use a medium concentric shaped coil for the majority of my nugget hunting.

Large Coils: Large coils are designed for maximum depth penetration and covering a wide search area. They are excellent for searching open areas where ground coverage is essential. These are a favorite in areas where trash targets are limited and there are seemingly limitless amounts of area to hunt. Large coils can detect deeper targets but they aren't as effective in separating closely spaced targets or in heavily trash-infested locations.

Apart from these three standard sizes, some manufacturers may offer specialized coils for specific purposes, such as:

Elliptical Coils: These coils have an elongated shape and offer improved maneuverability compared to round coils. They will get slightly less depth than a round coil of the same size, but they are useful for getting into tight spots, such as between rocks or under tree branches. I use elliptical coils for most of my detecting.

Super Large Coils: These are exceptionally large coils, often several feet in diameter, that are used by be detectorists seeking extreme depth. These may be an option if you are in an area you know to have very large nugget at depth, but their weight makes them very uncomfortable to hunt with for very long.

Waterproof Coils: Many metal detectors come with waterproof coils designed for use in shallow water or wet environments like beaches. Some advanced models even offer fully submersible coils for underwater metal detecting. This can be a nice feature if you are hunting bedrock adjacent to a creek or river, or actually scanning bedrock cracks underwater.

DD or Mono: Make note that detector coils will either be DD (Double-D) or Mono (Monoloop). The main difference between DD (Double-D) and Mono (Monoloop) coils on a metal detector lies in their design and performance characteristics. DD coils are excellent at canceling out ground mineralization and reducing interference from electromagnetic sources and offer more stable performance in highly mineralized soils and areas with a lot of metal debris. However, DD coils have noticeably less depth compared to mono coils, and they might not be as sensitive to small targets. In contrast, Mono coils are known for their increased sensitivity, especially to smaller targets and objects deep in the ground. They can provide better depth performance compared to DD coils, but they are generally more affected by ground mineralization and can experience increased interference in challenging environments.

The availability of different coil sizes may vary depending on the brand and model of the metal detector. Most detectors allow interchangeable coils, though some are hard-wired with just one coil. Most VLF detectors have at least a few different options, whereas others like pulse induction Minelab detectors have dozens of different coil options to choose from. Coil options are definitely a consideration to make before you purchase a detector.

Sticking with a Coil

Whichever detector/coil setup you decide to use, I would strongly encourage you find something that works and stick with it rather than constantly changing out coils. Becoming a proficient gold detectors requires you to understand the sounds your machine is making. Any adjustment you make (whether that's an change in settings, swapping out coils, or using a different detector completely) will require you to relearn the sounds that your detector is sending you.

I rarely change my detector coils. I have found a size that works for me in most of my hunting situations. I have used the same detector/coil combination for years and I have gotten very good at understanding the sounds that my detector is making. Yes, I do have a few different sizes of coils in my arsenal, and I do change them from time to time, but for 90% of my detecting I use the same setup. I'm confident that I find more gold because of it.

The Good and Bad of Discrimination

Most modern detectors have an iron discrimination feature that can help you separate ferrous targets (iron trash) from nonferrous targets (gold nuggets). Using the iron discrimination feature on a metal detector can have some major pros and cons, especially when detecting for gold nuggets. Let's explore them:

Pros:

1. **Eliminating Iron Junk**: Iron discrimination allows you to filter out signals from ferrous metals like nails, bottle caps, and other common iron junk items. This can save time and effort, as you won't need to dig up unwanted targets, especially in areas littered with iron debris. Some mining sites are incredibly trashy, making them nearly impossible to hunt without some way to discriminate out iron targets.

2. **Focus on Precious Metals**: By using discrimination, you can concentrate on detecting non-ferrous metals like gold, silver, copper and lead. Even with good discrimination, you will still dig **A LOT** of trash. Many sites are littered with lead pellets and bullets that sound indistinguishable from a gold nugget. You will need to dig these targets or risk losing gold. While discrimination can help you focus on the "good targets." You're still going to be digging a lot of rubbish, but it will cut down on some of the larger iron targets that you might encounter.

3. **Smoother Signal Response**: Discrimination can improve the detector's signal response by providing cleaner and more distinguishable signals for non-ferrous targets. This makes it easier to identify and differentiate valuable metals from unwanted iron objects. Unfortunately, this also reduces the detectors overall sensitivity considerably...

Cons:

1. **Potential to Miss Gold Nuggets**: Over-reliance on iron discrimination can cause you to miss small or deeply buried gold nuggets. Gold nuggets, especially smaller ones, can have similar conductivity to certain iron minerals, and excessive discrimination could filter out those signals.

2. **Depth and Sensitivity Reduction**: When using discrimination, the detector's overall depth and sensitivity will decrease, as it ignores a range of signals from certain metals. This could result in shallower

detection depth and potentially missing larger gold nuggets that are buried deeper in the ground. The difference is noticeable. You will miss a lot of gold if you run discrimination.

3. **Inaccurate Discrimination**: Discrimination settings are not perfect and can be prone to false positives or negatives. Even if you hear the signal, some gold nuggets may appear similar to iron or other metals, leading to incorrect discrimination and possibly digging up unwanted items or ignoring valuable targets.

4. **Missed Relics and other Valuables**: While the focus is on gold nuggets, you might miss other valuable artifacts or non-gold metal items that could be of interest. The early miners often camped right on their gold claims, so there may be some interesting relics that you might miss out on if you use discrimination.

Using iron discrimination on a metal detector can be helpful in certain situations, especially when dealing with highly iron-infested areas. However, when prospecting specifically for gold nuggets, sensitivity is usually much more important. Using iron discrimination will have a very negative impact on your detectors ability to find small gold, which is much more common that the bigger nuggets. In MOST situations, I recommend not using any discrimination. Most experienced gold hunters agree.

Hunting Trashy Sites with VLF Detectors and Small Coils

There is one situation where iron-discrimination is almost a requirement, and that is at sites that are absolutely infested with iron trash targets. Some sites are simply impossible to hunt effectively due to the amount of iron rubbish scattered throughout the site. In these situations, digging every target is simply not an option, as you could spend all day digging and never move farther that 20 feet.

Using a VLF metal detector with a small coil and good iron discrimination can allow you to selectively hunt these sites by ignoring the iron trash and focusing on the signals that are more likely to be gold.

1. **Elimination of Iron Junk**: One of the most significant advantages of using a VLF metal detector with good iron discrimination is its ability to filter out signals from ferrous metals like nails, bottle caps, and other common trash items. This feature saves valuable time and effort by reducing the need to dig up unwanted targets, allowing you to focus on potentially valuable non-ferrous targets like gold nuggets.
2. **Enhanced Target Identification**: VLF detectors with advanced iron discrimination features can provide more accurate and reliable target identification. They can distinguish between different types of metals, helping you identify gold nuggets more effectively among the clutter of trash targets. While the target ID is never guaranteed, most detectors

made now area actually pretty accurate at distinguishing between ferrous and nonferrous metals. You can ignore the iron targets and focus instead on the "good" nonferrous targets like lead, aluminum, brass, silver and gold.

3. **Customizable Settings**: Many VLF metal detectors with iron discrimination features allow you to adjust the discrimination level to suit the specific conditions of the site. This flexibility enables you to fine-tune the detector to the amount of trash targets present while still maintaining some sensitivity to smaller gold nuggets. This lets you strike a balance between filtering out unwanted signals and not missing potential gold targets.

By using a small coil you can significantly improve your experience while hunting trashy sites and improve your target recovery rate significantly. A common issue with these iron infested sites is that you will hear multiple targets under your coil at the same time.

Let's say, for example, that you are swinging a large 18" round coil. As you swing that big coil over a piece of ground, buried underneath the ground are 5 rusty square nails and a 1-gram gold nugget. Sensing this many different targets at the same time will likely confuse your detector and produce tones and target IDs that indicate iron targets. There's a good chance that you would walk right over the gold nugget.

With a small coil, you can search an area with much more precision. Rather than getting an overwhelming response from multiple targets, you can carefully scan the area. You'll have better odds of hearing that gold nugget among the trash.

It is essential to note that while iron discrimination can be beneficial in trashy areas, it's definitely not foolproof. There is always a risk of false positives or missing certain gold nuggets that have similar conductivity to iron or are deeply buried. As with any metal detecting, a balance between discrimination and sensitivity should be struck, and it's crucial to understand the capabilities and limitations of your metal detector to optimize your results.

Patch Hunting

Patch hunting involves using a metal detector to search areas not necessarily known to contain gold. Most people prospect for gold in known gold areas, searching the exact area that the old-timers worked with sluice boxes and drywashers many years ago.

Of course there is good reason to hunt for gold in these areas. the simple fact that gold has been found there in the past makes it very reasonable to believe that there is still some gold that was left behind. Throughout this book I have been stressing the importance of identifying past gold producing areas. Nearly all nugget shooters gravitate to these areas, as they can still be very productive. There have undoubtedly been many thousands of ounces of gold recovered with metal detectors in the past few decades by reworking these well documented gold sites.

The difficulty with reworking old mining ground is that many of these areas are no secret among gold miners. Most of the mining districts in the United States were originally worked in the mid-to-late 1800s, and again in the 1920s and 1930s during the Great Depression.

Since the advent of metal detector technology, many of these areas have been pounded. While nuggets can still be recovered from even the most hammered patches, it is a simple fact that most well-known gold districts have been hunted hard, and gold nuggets are getting harder and harder to find.

The difference with the method of patch hunting for gold nuggets is that you are actually seeking out new and undiscovered gold deposits that have never been found. We are talking about virgin ground; areas that have perhaps never been searched with a metal detector before.

There are benefits and drawbacks of this gold prospecting method. The biggest drawback (and the reason that few people hunt for gold this way) is the fact that even the best patch hunters have to endure long dry spells, where they find no gold at all. Gold is rare, and finding an undiscovered patch of gold nuggets is no easy task. While metal detecting the well-known areas is getting less and less productive, a skilled detectorist can usually still squeak out a nugget now and then. When patch hunting, you are likely to endure days, weeks, maybe even months without finding any gold.

The potential benefit of patch hunting for gold nuggets is obvious. When you do find some gold, you are the first person to find it. Unlike so many gold mining areas that have been hunted by hundreds or even thousands of prospectors, the discovery is all yours. It takes a huge amount of patience and persistence, but the potential for a nice payoff could be very good.

So what is the best way to start patch hunting? **Although successful patch hunters are exploring new ground, don't believe for a second that they are wandering aimlessly!** In fact, successful patch hunters extensively research the areas that they are prospecting. They can't be certain that they will find gold, but they are absolutely searching in a way that will increase their odds. Without research, there is almost zero chance of success.

To properly research areas to patch hunt for gold, there are two very important considerations. One of these considerations is nearby mining gold mining activity. Yes, we are talking about discovering new deposits of gold, but this does not mean that we are searching hundreds of miles away from any known districts. To the contrary, most gold patches will be found very close to well-known areas, often on the fringes of these areas. This may be several miles away, or it may be as nearby as one drainage away. We aren't searching for the next gold rush, we are just looking for undiscovered small patches, and these are often on the fringes of known gold areas.

The other aspect of research that is critical for the successful patch hunter is to understand geology and the nature of how gold is formed and deposited in the natural environment. The different types of placer deposits in an area will influence how a patch hunter searches with their metal detector. In much of the Southwestern U.S., Eolian gold placers dominate the landscape, which are often deposited very close to the surface and easily found with a metal detector. Other types of placer gold deposits will require different search methods. An extensive understanding of where and how gold is naturally deposited across the landscape that you are hunting in is critical to the success of a patch hunter.

Patch hunting for gold is not for everyone. The amount of patience and persistence required to successfully find new deposits of gold using this method will test anyone's limits, but if you can stay focused and put in a lot of hours and hard work you may just be rewarded with many ounces of gold.

Gridding

Gridding is a systematic method used when searching with a handheld metal detector, typically employed in scenarios where you want to thoroughly search and area and ensure that you find every target. Gridding is the opposite of patch hunting. Rather than moving fast and covering a large area, you area going to slow down and systematically "dissect" an area, ensuring that you've searched it to the best of your abilities.

The process is almost always reserved for areas where gold has already been found. You've already detected several nuggets in a relatively small area, and you want to thoroughly cover it to make sure you find all the gold.

Let's say for example that you dug up two nuggets a few feet apart. This would be a good indication that there is more gold in the vicinity. I will mark out an area approximately 30' x 30'. Every few feet (about the width of my coil swing) I will tie a small piece of fluorescent orange tape onto a bush.

Now I will start in the corner and work my way strait across in a straight line toward to flagging directly across from me. Go slow and methodically, working your coil carefully around the grass and bushes, but make sure you work in a straight line across the grid. When you get to the end, move over a few feet to the next piece of flagging and work back across to the next piece of flagging.

The result of gridding is that you can cover an area very effectively, ensuring that you don't miss anything. If you have confidence in the area and are finding gold, I suggest doing the same zig-zag pattern again at a 90 degree angle from the first grid. You will be surprised at how well gold can hide among the rocks, grass and bushes. Hunting an area methodically from different directions can help to put more gold in your poke at the end of the day.

Hunting Small Gold on Bedrock

Exposed bedrock is the ideal place to search for gold with your metal detector as it can only penetrate short distance into the ground. Many rich areas have significant overburden that do not allow the gold beneath them to be detected. Even the best metal detector is unable to find a nugget that is covered with several feet of overburden. Gold deposits on exposed bedrock are either right at or just below the surface so your metal detector will be quite useful when searching in these areas.

Bedrock is part of the top layer of the crust of the Earth and there are countless different varieties that make up its composition. In gold country, granite, slate, serpentine and schist are just some types that are commonly found.

However, even more important than the composition is the actual texture of the surface of bedrock. Some bedrock types are very smooth and do not catch and trap gold very well. A rougher textured bedrock is more likely to hold gold nuggets within the cracks.

When using your metal detector to find gold, rough textured bedrock is your best bet. This is because rough bedrock with plenty of cracks makes a natural location for gold to be captured and held for you to find with your detector. During ancient times when a stream or river passed over the area, the gold that traveled downstream would get caught in the cracks of bedrock and remain stuck in place. The same happens with natural erosion and gravitational movement of gold downhill. It will continue to move downhill until something captures and holds it. Rough textured bedrock does this perfectly.

Exposed bedrock like this is perfect for a sensitive VLF metal detector paired with a small concentric coil.

Using your metal detector in the rough patches of bedrock will help you find the gold. Your metal detector should be sensitive enough to detect very small nuggets, as this is primarily what you will find.

Simply pass your metal detector in a slow, sweep pattern just above the surface and be sure to cover the area carefully as it is easy to miss the sound of small pieces of gold. Scan slowly, scan from different directions and angles. A small concentric coil usually works best, allowing you put the tip of the coil down into narrow cracks and search efficiently among the rocks.

The placer gold will usually be lodged in the cracks, so be sure to carry a few tools with you to pry out the gold once your metal detector has located it.

While some gold may be staring up at you all exposed on the surface, in all likelihood you will have to do a little digging and prying in order to extract the gold from its location. Most of the time you will only find very small pieces but occasionally you might hit larger nuggets that have gone undetected for many years all because others before you didn't quite pass over that spot.

Efficient Target Recovery

One thing that is rarely discussed is the importance of efficient target recovery when metal detecting. Target recovery is simply the process of digging a target out of the ground. Efficiently recovering a target from the ground when metal detecting is essential to preserve the integrity of the find, prevent damage to the target, and minimize disturbance to the surrounding area.

Once you decide that you're going to dig a target, you want to get it out as quickly as possible. Speed and efficiency is important because it will increase the amount of gold you find. Digging lots of trash is just a part of gold detecting, and even if you choose to be selective about the targets you dig, you will still dig WAY MORE trash targets than gold nuggets.

On an average day of nugget hunting, I am likely to dig anywhere from fifty to several hundred metal targets. If I am lucky, a few of those targets will be gold. The quicker you can get the target out of the ground and move on to the next, the more gold you're going to find.

The speed of recovery will usually depend on how deep the average target depth is. If I am hunting deep targets with my PI detector and I am commonly digging holes that are 1 or 2 feet deep, I will definitely dig less targets than if I'm hunting shallow ground where targets are only a few inches deep.

Here is my method for quickly digging a target:

1. I like to have a pretty good idea of where the target is before I start digging. To do this, I swing my coil over the target from several different angles, noting where the sound is the loudest. In my mind, I will visualize an "X" as I swing the coil from one direction and then the other, noting where it is loudest. This gives me an idea of where the target is so I know where to dig. This method is especially important when you are hunting deeper targets and using larger coils.

2. Digging Technique: Use a digging tool appropriate for the terrain. For most nugget hunting that means a good quality pick with a sharp digging end and a flatter scraping end. If I am using a VLF detector to hunting shallower targets, I prefer a shorter, lighter pick. If I am using a PI detector and I anticipate deeper targets, I use a heavy pick with a 30" handle. When digging, use caution to dig beyond the target and scrape back toward you as you excavate the hole. The last thing you want to do is strike down directly on top of a nugget, as you might scratch it and destroy its collectible value.

3. Pinpointing: Some prospectors prefer to use a handheld pinpointer to search their dig hole once they start getting close to their target. I mainly prefer to just use the coil of my detector and scan the hole as I dig and reevaluate where I think the target is located.

4. The Final Recovery: When you get close to the target, set your metal detector down on the ground and use a plastic scoop to dig out small amounts of soil and scan it over the top of your coil. **Scan the soil over your coil, not the other way around.** This is much more effective and less clumsy than moving your coil around. When you finally get the nugget in your scoop, carefully pour half of the soil into your free hand. Scan the scoop over the coil again. If the target is there, you can toss your handful and pour half into your hand again. If the target is in your hand, pour out the scoop and put half of the soil from your hand back into the scoop. Do this process of halving the dirt repeatedly, until you've narrowed down your target.

5. After you've recovered your target, **fill in your hole!** Please don't be lazy about this... take a few extra seconds to properly fill the hole.

Dealing with Trash

Metal "trash" items are an unavoidable part of metal detecting. Even under the best conditions you are going to find WAY MORE non-gold items than you will gold nuggets.

Even hunting some of the most remote goldfields, you will be surprised just how much "junk" there is in the ground. The early miners didn't have garbage service, so every piece of metal rubbish the accumulated was tossed aside.

Dealing with trash is without a doubt one of the most frustrating aspects of metal detecting for gold nuggets. Since many of the best gold bearing areas across the west have been previously worked by prospectors, there is a lot of rubbish to deal with. The miners who hunted for gold a century ago weren't as conscious of leaving garbage behind like we are today.

This historic image of an old mining camp in Colorado beautifully illustrates why we find so much metal rubbish today!

Nearly all of the old placer grounds that you will encounter today will have an abundance of junk, ranging from tiny boot tacks and square nails to shovel heads and huge 30-gallon oil drums. As the past century-and-a-half has passed, more and more modern garbage has accumulated; beer cans, bullets, shell casings, and just about anything else you can imagine will show up.

The problem only gets worse when items rust apart. A section of thin metal that was in one piece 100 years ago may be scattered into a thousand small bits today, giving your detector fits.

Thoughts on Digging All Targets

One thing I have been told by countless gold hunters over the years is the importance of digging ALL targets regardless of the sound that your detector makes, or the ID number on the screen (on detectors that have visual indicators). Since discrimination is never 100% accurate, the only way to ensure you aren't walking over gold is to dig everything you hear.

Whether you are willing to admit it or not, most gold prospectors have had days when they do some selective digging. After a long hot day of digging holes, it's only natural to get a little sloppy. That big, booming target that you just know is a beer can for example. You just walk past it...

So did you just walk by the target of a lifetime? It is absolutely possible that you did. A 20-ounce gold nugget probably sounds exactly like a beer can or any other large chunk of metal. I don't even want to think about how many thousands of big trash targets there are for every multi-ounce gold nugget there are out there.

If you want to make sure that doesn't ever happen to you, then yes, you'd better dig all targets. There's just no way to know for sure what is buried under the ground until you dig it up.

Still, sometimes I am selective about the targets that I dig. Here are a few situations where I might not dig every target...

I am using a VLF detector and I am getting a repeating "iron" indication

Most VLF detectors today have pretty accurate discrimination, particularly for decent sized iron targets. If I am in an area with quite a bit of iron trash, and my target ID is giving a repeating and constant indication of iron, I might very well pass by it without digging. I can be pretty confident that it isn't gold. However, if the target ID is bouncing around and inconsistent, I will definitely dig.

My detector is giving an OVERLOAD signal

Most detectors now have a feature that gives an overload signal on really big targets. Big chunks of steel, beer cans, railroad spikes, etc. Yes, it could be a gigantic gold nugget, but in all honesty I often walk past the overload signals.

You see lots of iron trash on the surface of the ground

Sometimes you will walk into a big patch of targets and your detector will start going crazy because there are multiple targets with every swing. Closer inspection might show that there is a rotting piece of sheet metal and bits of iron scattered around the surface. Those targets you are hearing are just bits of iron that have rotted off the bigger chunk. I walk past these places, because otherwise I would spend all day just digging junk.

The target is big, but the gold nuggets are small

You should know the area that you are prospecting. Some areas simply don't produce large gold nuggets, and only have smaller flakes and picker sized gold. If you get a big, booming target you can be pretty confident that it is a piece of trash, since small gold will give a mellow, smoother signal.

I'm tired

Yeah, I'm kind of joking here, but the truth is after a long day in the sun, I just might get a bit lazier than I am going to be at the start of the day. If the target gives some indication that it probably isn't gold, I might just move on. Yes, this is probably bad advice and you should dig that target. If you find yourself getting a bit sloppy late in the day you are probably better off to find some shade or maybe head back to camp for a few hours, drink some water and get your focus back.

Overall, I agree with the consensus that you should dig all metal targets while you are metal detecting. It is the only way to be absolutely sure that you aren't missing any gold, and being selective about what you dig will without a doubt make you miss some gold eventually.

However, the other consideration is how much time you are spending digging after those pieces of trash? If you are 99% sure that you are digging another square nail, and you are going to spend 5 or 10 minutes getting it out of the ground, perhaps your time is better spend hunting onward and passing by that signal? This is something I don't see discussed very often, but we only have so much time in the day, and *it may be more efficient to be selective with your digging time to increase the odds of putting your coil over top of a gold nugget.*

Just remember, most of us aren't gold prospecting to make a living, we are doing it because we enjoy it and want to have a good time. If you have a prospecting style that you prefer, then by all means do it. Ultimately, if you are finding gold nuggets then you are doing it right!

Hearing gold among all the chatter (trash is LOUD, nuggets are Quiet)

Dealing with both iron trash objects and hot rocks is by far the biggest challenge that any gold nugget hunter has to deal with. I wish that there was some huge secret that I could tell you that would help you deal with it, but the simple truth is that there are no real shortcuts.

Hot rocks have a different amount of mineralization than the surrounding soil, so a well-tuned machine is going to notice them with a faint target response. These can be most apparent in areas with a mix of different host rock materials. Pulse Induction metal detectors are much better at ignoring hot rocks, whereas many VLF detectors will sound off on every one.

A hot rock will usually be found on or near the surface. The signal from a hot rock will usually be strongest immediately under the coil. Lift the coil up even an inch or two and the signal will weaken or disappear considerably.

You are also likely to encounter areas with hot ground, not exactly hot rocks, but an area where mineral rich soils set off your detector. This can be confusing at first, but easily recognizable with experience.

Trash targets, both ferrous and non-ferrous, may be less confusing than dealing with mineralized ground and hot rocks, but that doesn't mean it's not frustrating to deal with. Trashy areas can cause your detector to hit on so many different signals it can really be defeating after a while. With experience, you may choose to ignore some of the obvious iron signals, but lead bullets and small non-ferrous targets should not be ignored and need to be dug.

The best advice I can give to anyone is to learn your detector; understand the different tones and responses that it makes when out in the field. There are some things that you simply can't learn from a book. Understanding your detector requires lots of hours in the field. When you are digging a target, make a mental note of what it sounded like. After you have dug enough trash and hot rocks to fill your pockets, you will start to notice that there are minor differences in the type of response that your machine makes compared to gold nuggets.

Listening for Small and Deep Targets

I hate to be the bearer of bad news, but there are very few large nuggets that are shallow these days. Except for perhaps the most remote goldfields on Earth, those easy nuggets are long gone. If you want to develop a touch of envy, just talk to a detectorist who hunted for gold in the 1980s and hear stories of all the nuggets they would find just inches from the surface of the ground.

No doubt there are still a few whopper nuggets sitting at shallow depths even today, for the most part the modern gold hunter is primarily focused on two types of gold; small nuggets, and larger nuggets that are so deep that they have been missed by previous detectorists.

Experienced gold hunters have a saying... Go "Slow and Low." What this means is that you move slowly and methodically when detecting for gold. Keep your detector coil low to the ground. Go slowly and carefully, maneuvering around rocks, grass and shrubs.

A fast, aggressive swing won't find you gold. You'll hear big trash targets, but you will swing right over those smaller, deeper nuggets without hearing a sound. Go SLOW and keep the coil LOW to the ground.

Very few gold targets nowadays give a big loud signal. You need to be focused on the faint, repeating signals. Even small breaks in the threshold hum of your detector might be the only indication you will get on a deep target. Eventually, you need to learn to hear the targets that 99% of other detectorists have missed. That is the secret to finding gold in 2020 and beyond.

Using Handheld Pinpointers

Handheld pinpointers have become fairly popular in recent years. I consider them optional, but in certain situations a small handheld pinpointer can help you to recover targets more quickly.

Years ago, prospectors considered these to be pretty much worthless for nugget hunting, but some recent models that have come out that work quite well.

I carry one with me, but I find that I don't use it very often because it just isn't necessary most of the time. I would recommend that you learn to be proficient with target recovery using your detector coil.

Fill your HOLES!

One of the quickest ways to lose access to an area is to leave holes unfilled. I'm still blown away by the laziness of some detectorists when I see giant craters left behind by others.

It takes seconds to fill a hole back in. Do it every time.

Get Lots of Time in the Field

You can read every book available about metal detecting, but ultimately what will make you a truly effective nugget hunter is time in the field. There is no short cut to experience. Study and research can definitely increase your odds off success by helping to put you in the right areas to find gold, but when it comes to learning the "language" of your detector, you've got to put in the hours.

Most effective nugget hunters will tell that it took them many years to become proficient at metal detecting for gold. I spent many months and dozens of trips out in the field before I found my first nugget. I'm not alone either. Many successful detectorists had a similar experience.

Pushing past the frustration and continuing to hunt takes determination. I would bet money that 95% of the people that buy a gold detector never find a single gold nugget, and probably don't even use it more than a few times. They go out in the field and hunt a few times, give up and find a new hobby.

Joining Prospecting Clubs

I would recommend that you seek out a local prospecting club in your area. All throughout the country there are prospecting clubs. Most of them have club claims, which provide access to claims for members. Joining them is usually pretty inexpensive.

These claims are usually worked over pretty hard, but it's a great way to get started if you don't have a place to prospect and you're just getting started.

The real benefit of joining a club is meeting fellow prospectors. For most, gold prospecting is a solitary activity. In some areas, it would be quite possible to prospect for years and never meet another prospector out in the field. Actively seeking out local prospecting clubs is a great way to meet other prospectors to learn from.

Online Forums

Online forums are another way to meet fellow prospectors. For detectorists, this can be beneficial because you can find folks that are specifically into gold detecting.

I've found that for the most part, local clubs are comprised of placer miners that are focused mostly on panning, sluicing, dredging, highbanking, etc. Not to say those folks don't have good knowledge about finding gold in general, they aren't necessarily experienced with metal detectors. With forums and Facebook Groups, you will find prospectors with a specific interest in nugget hunting.

I have several friends that I go metal detecting with that I first met online through the forums. They are a great way to connect with like-minded individuals in a way that wasn't available to previous generations.

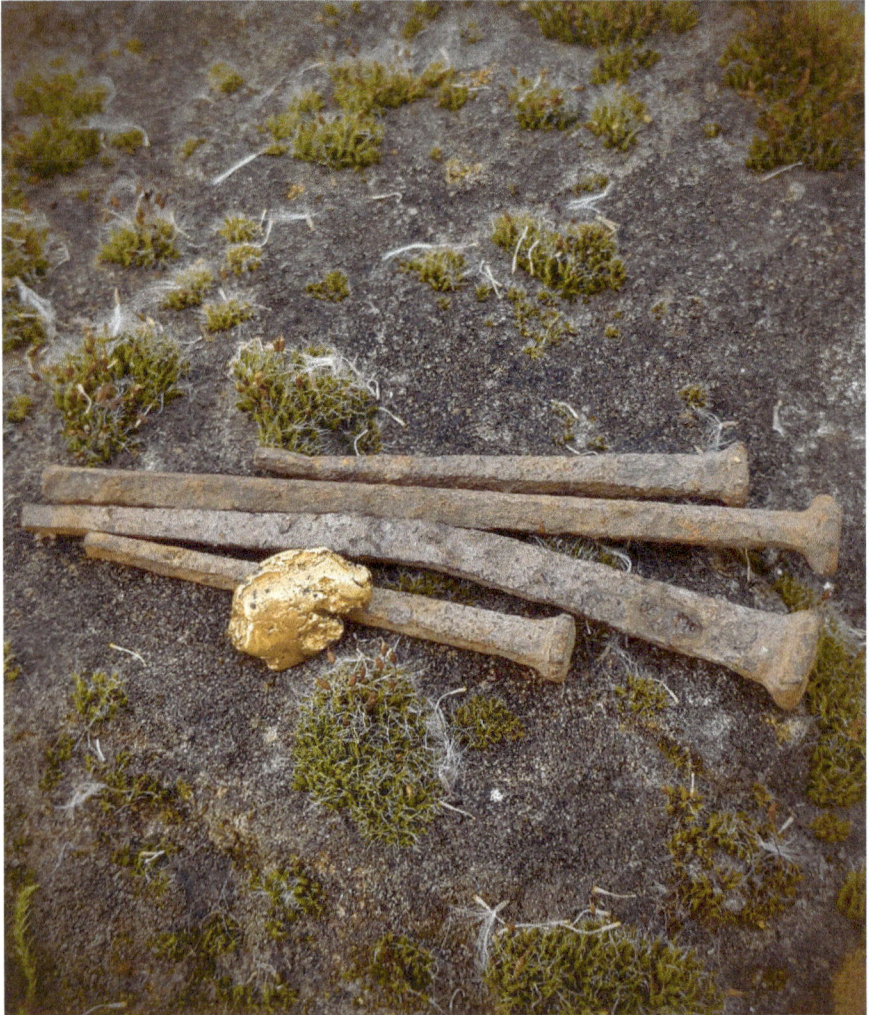

Conclusion

Enjoy the Adventure!

Make no mistake... metal detecting for gold nuggets is hard work. I have seen countless newcomers come and go in this hobby. Everyone likes the idea of digging up treasure, but when the reality sets of just how much work is involved, most of them move on. It's the rare person that can put in the work to be truly successful.

I have tried my best to help to set realistic expectations while writing this book. I have met and spoken to some of the most successful nugget hunters in the US. Nearly all of them would agree that detecting for gold nuggets, especially now in the 2020s and beyond, isn't easy. Most of the "easy" gold has been found, and it doesn't grow back.

"Gold Fever" is very real, and the allure of hidden gold can take you to some amazing places. I have hunted for gold in several different states, and seen some incredible country far off the beaten path that few others have seen. The dream to find that next big nugget keeps me going, even on the hardest days. Focus *more* on the adventures you will have and the places that you will find, and focus *less* on the gold. If I wasn't a gold prospector, I would still he a fisherman, a hiker, a hunter. Detecting for gold is an excuse for me to get out and enjoy the outdoors. The gold is simply a bonus.

www.ingramcontent.com/pod-product-compliance
Lightning Source LLC
Chambersburg PA
CBHW051729020426
42333CB00014B/1221